STATUTORY INSTRUMENTS

2005 No. 3281

AGRICULTURE

The Feeding Stuffs (England) Regulations 2005

Made - - - -	*28th November 2005*
Laid before Parliament	*5th December 2005*
Coming into force - -	*1st January 2006*

ARRANGEMENT OF REGULATIONS

PART 1

Introductory and General

1. Title, commencement and application
2. Interpretation
3. Modification of the Agriculture Act 1970 in relation to all feeding stuffs
4. Modification of the Agriculture Act 1970 in relation to imported feeding stuffs
5. Prescribed material to which requirements for the statutory statement and marking apply
6. Exemption from these Regulations
7. Revocations

PART 2

Presentation and Composition of Feeding Stuffs

8. Matters required and permitted to be contained in a statutory statement or otherwise declared
9. Forms of statutory statement
10. Limits of variation
11. Assigned meanings for statutory statements or marks
12. Manner of packaging and sealing compound feeding stuffs
13. Control of feed materials
14. Control of products intended for animal feed containing undesirable substances
15. Control of feeding stuffs containing prohibited materials
16. Control of certain protein sources
17. Control of the iron content of milk replacer feeds
18. Control of ash insoluble in hydrochloric acid in compound feeding stuffs

19. Control of feeding stuffs intended for particular nutritional purposes, and supplementary provisions relating to statutory statement

20. Control of additives and premixtures

21. Saving relating to confidential information relating to additives under the 2000 Regulations

PART 3

Enforcement

22. Enforcement of provisions made under section 2(2) of the European Communities Act 1972

23. Modification of section 74A(3) of the Agriculture Act 1970

PART 4

Amendments to other legislation

24. Amendments to the Feeding Stuffs (Sampling and Analysis) Regulations 1999

SCHEDULES

1. Method of calculating the energy value of compound feeds

2. Control of feed materials

   PART I—Principal processes used for the preparation of the feed materials listed in Part II of this Schedule

   PART II—Non-exclusive list of the main feed materials

   PART III—Other feed materials

3. Contents of the statutory statement or other declaration (except for additives and premixtures not contained in feeding stuffs)

   PART I

   PART II—Declaration of analytical constituents

4. Limits of variation

   PART A—Compound feeding stuffs except those for pets

   PART B—Compound pet foods

   PART C—Feed materials

   PART D—Vitamins and trace elements

   PART E—Energy value of compound feeding stuffs

5. Prescribed limits for undesirable substances

6. Control of certain protein sources

7. Permitted feeding stuffs intended for particular nutritional purposes and provisions relating to their use

8. Categories of feed materials for use in relation to compound feeding stuffs for pet animals

9. Amending instruments revoked

The Secretary of State makes the following Regulations in exercise of the powers conferred by sections 66(1), 68(1) and (1A), 69(1) and (3), 70(1), 71(1), 74(1), 74A, 77(4), 78(6) and (10), 79(1), (2) and (9), and 84 of the Agriculture Act 1970(a) (as read with regulation 14 of the Food Standards Act 1999 (Transitional and Consequential Provisions and Savings) (England and Wales) Regulations 2000(b) and with Articles 2 and 6 of the Ministry of Agriculture, Fisheries and Food (Dissolution) Order 2002)(c).

In so far as these Regulations cannot be made under the powers in the Agriculture Act 1970 specified above, the Secretary of State makes these Regulations in exercise of her powers as a Minister designated(d) for the purposes of section 2(2) of the European Communities Act 1972(e) in relation to the common agricultural policy of the European Community and measures in the veterinary and phytosanitary fields for the protection of public health.

There has been consultation in accordance with the requirements of section 84(1) of the Agriculture Act 1970 or as appropriate of Article 9 of Regulation (EC) No. 178/2002 of the European Parliament and of the Council laying down the general principles and requirements of food law, establishing the European Food Safety Authority and laying down procedures in matters of food safety(f).

PART 1

Introductory and General

Title, commencement and application

1.   These Regulations may be cited as the Feeding Stuffs (England) Regulations 2005, come into force on 1st January 2006 and apply in relation to England only.

Interpretation

2.—(1) In these Regulations—

"the Act" means the Agriculture Act 1970;

"additive", subject to regulation 21(4), means a feed additive to which the Additives Regulation applies, with the exception of any additive in categories (d) or (e) of Article 6(1) of that Regulation other than those in the functional groups listed in paragraph 4(a), (b) and (c) of Annex 1 to that Regulation;

"the Additives Directive" means Council Directive 70/524/EEC concerning additives in feeding stuffs(g);

"the Additives Regulation" means Regulation (EC) No. 1831/2003 of the European Parliament and of the Council on additives for use in animal nutrition(h);

"ash" means the matter which results from the treatment of a feeding stuff in accordance with the appropriate procedure set out in the method of analysis for ash specified in Point 5 of the Annex to Directive 71/250/EEC(i);

"the Certain Products Directive" means Council Directive 82/471/EEC concerning certain products used in animal nutrition(j);

(a) 1970 c. 40. Section 66(1) contains definitions of the expressions "the Ministers", "prescribed" and "regulations"; the definition of "the Ministers" was amended by the Transfer of Functions (Wales) (No. 1) Order 1978 (S.I. 1978/272), Schedule 5, paragraph 1. Functions of "the Ministers", so far as exercisable in relation to Wales, were transferred to the National Assembly for Wales by S.I. 1999/672. Those functions, so far as exercisable in relation to Scotland, were transferred to the Scottish Ministers by section 53 of the Scotland Act 1998 (1998 c. 46). By virtue of S.I. 1999/3141, functions of the Secretaries of State for Wales and Scotland previously exercisable in relation to England ceased to be so exercisable and were transferred to the Minister of Agriculture, Fisheries and Food. Section 74A was inserted by the European Communities Act 1972 (1972 c. 68), Schedule 4, paragraph 6.
(b) S.I. 2000/656.
(c) S.I. 2002/794.
(d) S.I. 1972/1811 in relation to the common agricultural policy and S.I. 1999/2027 in relation to measures in the veterinary and phytosanitary fields for the protection of public health.
(e) 1972 C. 68.
(f) OJ No. L31, 1.2.2002, p. 1, as last amended by Regulation (EC) No. 1642/2003 of the European Parliament and of the Council (OJ No. L245, 29.9.2003, p. 4).
(g) OJ No. L270, 14.12.70, p. 1 (OJ/SE Vol. 18, p. 4) last amended by Council Directive 1999/20/EC (OJ No. L80, 25.3.1999, p. 20).
(h) OJ No. L268, 18.10.2003, p. 29. Last amended by Commission Regulation (EC) No 378/2005 (OJ No. L59, 5.3.2005, p. 8).
(i) OJ No. L155, 12.7.71, p. 13 (OJ/SE 1971(II), p. 480).
(j) OJ No. L213, 21.7.82, p. 8. Last amended by Commission Directive 2004/116/EC (OJ No. L379, 24.12.2004, p. 81).

"complementary feeding stuff" means a compound feeding stuff which has a high content of certain substances and which, by reason of its composition, is sufficient for a daily ration only if it is used in combination with other feeding stuffs;

"complete feeding stuff" means a compound feeding stuff which, by reason of its composition, is sufficient for a daily ration;

"compound feeding stuff", subject to regulation 14(6), means a mixture of feed materials, whether or not containing any additive, for oral feeding to pet animals or farmed creatures in the form of complementary feeding stuffs or complete feeding stuffs;

"the Compound Feedingstuffs Directive" means Council Directive 79/373/EEC on the circulation of compound feedingstuffs(**a**);

"daily ration" means the average total quantity of feeding stuff, expressed on a 12% moisture basis, required daily by an animal of a given kind, age group and level of production in order to satisfy all its nutritional needs;

"EEA State" means a Member State, Norway, Iceland or Liechtenstein;

"energy value" means the energy value of a compound feeding stuff calculated in accordance with the relevant method specified in Schedule 1;

"establishment" has the meaning given by Article 3(d) of Regulation (EC) No. 183/2005 of the European Parliament and of the Council laying down requirements for feed hygiene(**b**);

"fat" means the extract obtained following the treatment of a feeding stuff in accordance with the appropriate procedure set out in the method of analysis for oils and fats specified in Part IV of the Annex to Directive 71/393/EEC(**c**);

"feeding stuff intended for a particular nutritional purpose" means a compound feeding stuff, the composition or method of manufacture of which distinguishes it from other feeding stuffs and from the type of products covered by Council Directive 90/167/EEC laying down the conditions governing the preparation, placing on the market and use of medicated feeding stuffs in the Community(**d**), and in respect of which any indication is given that it is intended for a particular nutritional purpose;

"feed material" means—

(a) any product of vegetable or animal origin, in its natural state, fresh or preserved;

(b) any product derived from such a product by industrial processing; or

(c) any organic or inorganic substance,

(whether or not containing any additive) and for use in oral feeding to pet animals or farmed creatures, directly as such, or after processing, in the preparation of a compound feeding stuff or as a carrier of a premixture;

"the Feed Materials Directive" means Council Directive 96/25/EC on the circulation of feed materials(**e**);

"fibre" means the organic matter calculated following the treatment of a feeding stuff in accordance with the procedure set out in the method of analysis for fibre specified in Point 3 of Annex 1 to Directive 73/46/EEC(**f**);

"mammalian meat and bone meal" has the meaning given in Regulation 3(1) of the TSE (England) Regulations 2002(**g**);

"Member State" means a Member State other than the United Kingdom;

"micro-organism" has the meaning given by Article 2(2)(m) of the Additives Regulation;

"milk replacer feed" means a compound feeding stuff administered in dry form, or after reconstitution with a given quantity of liquid, for feeding young animals as a supplement to, or substitute for, post-colostral milk or for feeding calves intended for slaughter;

"mineral feeding stuff" means a complementary feeding stuff which is composed mainly of minerals and which contains at least 40% by weight of ash;

(**a**) OJ No. L86, 6.4.79, p. 30. Last amended by Council Regulation (EC) No 807/2003 (OJ No. L122, 16.5.2003, p. 36).
(**b**) OJ No. L35, 8.2.2005, p. 1.
(**c**) OJ No. L279, 20.12.71, p. 7 (OJ/SE 1971(III), p. 987). (Part IV was replaced entirely by Annex 1 to Directive 84/4/EEC (OJ No. L15. 18.1.84, p. 28. That Annex was in turn replaced entirely by Part B of the Annex to Directive 98/64/EC (OJ No. L257, 19.9.98, p. 14)).
(**d**) OJ No. L92, 7.4.90, p. 42.
(**e**) OJ No. L125, 23.5.96, p. 35. Last amended by Council Regulation (EC) No. 806/2003 (OJ No. L122, 16.5.2003, p. 1).
(**f**) OJ No. L83, 30.3.73, p. 21. (Point 3 of Annex 1 was replaced entirely by the Annex to Directive 92/89/EEC) (OJ No. L344, 26.11.92, p. 35)).
(**g**) S.I. 2002/843, as amended by S.I. 2002/1253, S.I. 2002/2860, S.I. 2003/1482 and S.I. 2004/1518.

"minimum storage life" means, in relation to a compound feeding stuff, the date until which, under proper storage conditions, that feeding stuff retains its specific properties;

"molassed feeding stuff" means a complementary feeding stuff prepared from molasses and which contains at least 14% by weight of total sugar expressed as sucrose;

"moisture" means water and other volatile material determined in accordance with the procedure set out in the method of analysis for moisture specified in Part I of the Annex to Directive 71/393/EEC(**a**);

"oil" means the extract obtained following the treatment of a feeding stuff in accordance with the appropriate procedure set out in the method of analysis for oils and fats specified in Part IV of the Annex to Directive 71/393/EEC(**b**);

"particular nutritional purpose" means the purpose of satisfying any nutritional requirement of pet animals or productive livestock, the process of assimilation or absorption of which, or the metabolism of which, may be temporarily impaired, or is temporarily or permanently impaired, and which may therefore benefit from ingestion of a feeding stuff capable of achieving that purpose;

"pet food" means a feeding stuff for pet animals and "compound pet food" shall be construed accordingly;

"premixture" has the meaning given by Article 2(2)(e) of the Additives Regulation, excluding any premixture consisting solely of feed additives in categories (d) or (e) of Article 6(1) of that Regulation, other than those in the functional groups listed in paragraph 4(a), (b) and (c) of Annex 1 to that Regulation;

"prescribed material" means material described in regulation 5(1);

"product intended for animal feed" means any product used or intended for use in feed for pet animals, farmed creatures or animals living freely in the wild;

"protein", except in paragraphs 7(2), 8, 9 and 10 of Part I of Schedule 3 where it has the meaning given to it by regulation 3(1) of the TSE (England) Regulations 2002(**c**), means the matter obtained as a result of treatment of a feeding stuff in accordance with the procedure set out in the method of analysis for protein specified in Point 2 of Annex 1 to Directive 72/199/EEC(**d**);

"put into circulation" means sell or otherwise transfer, have in possession with a view to selling or otherwise transferring, or offer for sale, in each case to a third party, and in regulations 13(8) and 14 also means import into England from a state other than an EEA State;

"starch" means the matter obtained as the result of treatment of a feeding stuff in accordance with the procedure set out in the method of analysis for starch specified in Point 1 of Annex 1 to Directive 72/199/EEC(**e**);

"2000 Regulations" means the Feeding Stuffs Regulations 2000(**f**);

"undesirable substance" means any substance or product, not being a pathogenic agent, which is present in or on a product intended for animal feed and—

(a) constitutes a potential danger to animal or human health or the environment; or

(b) could adversely affect livestock production.

(2) Any reference in these Regulations to a numbered regulation or Schedule shall, unless the context otherwise requires, be construed as a reference to the regulation or Schedule bearing that number in these Regulations.

(**a**) OJ No. L279, 20.12.71, p. 7 (OJ/SE 1971(III), p. 987), amended by Article 1 of Directive 73/47/EEC (OJ No. L83, 30.3.73, p. 35).

(**b**) OJ No. L279, 20.12.71, p. 7 (OJ/SE 1971(III), p. 987). (Part IV was replaced entirely by Annex 1 to Directive 84/4/EEC (OJ No. L15. 18.1.84, p. 28). That Annex was in turn replaced entirely by Part B of the Annex to Directive 98/64/EC (OJ No. L257, 19.9.98, p. 14).

(**c**) S.I. 2002/843, as amended by S.I. 2002/1253, S.I. 2002/2860, S.I. 2003/1482 and S.I. 2004/1518.

(**d**) OJ No. L123, 29.5.72, p. 6 (OJ/SE 1966-1972 supplement, p. 74), (Point 2 of Annex 1 has been replaced by the Annex to Directive 93/28/EEC (OJ No. L179, 22.7.93, p. 8)).

(**e**) OJ No. L123, 29.5.72, p. 6 (OJ/SE 1966-1972 supplement, p. 74), (Point 1 of Annex 1 has been replaced entirely by the Annex to Directive 1999/79/EC (OJ No. L209, 7.8.1999, p. 23)).

(**f**) S.I. 2000/2481, as last amended by S.I. 2004/2688.

(3) Where, in any tabular or other entry in a Schedule to these Regulations, a numbered reference to a footnote appears, the footnote so numbered shall be treated as included in or amplifying the text to which it relates.

(4) Any reference in these Regulations to a numbered section shall, unless otherwise indicated, be construed as a reference to the section bearing that number in the Act.

(5) Any reference in these Regulations to a Community instrument shall be construed as a reference to that instrument as amended on the date that these Regulations are made.

Modification of the Agriculture Act 1970 in relation to all feeding stuffs

3.—(1) Subsection (1) of section 66 shall have effect in England as if—
    (a) for the definition of "feeding stuff" there were substituted the following definition—
        ""feeding stuff" means—
        (a) a product of vegetable or animal origin in its natural state (whether fresh or preserved);
        (b) a product derived from the industrial processing of such a product; or
        (c) an organic or inorganic substance, used singly or in a mixture,
    whether or not containing additives, for oral feeding to pet animals or farmed creatures;";
    (b) for the definition of "pet animal" there were substituted the following definition—
        ""pet animal" means an animal belonging to a species normally nourished and kept, but not consumed, by man, other than an animal bred for fur;".

(2) Subsection (2) of section 66 shall have effect in England as if the following were substituted for paragraph (b) of that subsection—
    "(b) material shall be treated—
        (i) as imported or sold for use as a feeding stuff whether it is imported or, as the case may be, sold, to be used by itself, or as an ingredient in something which is to be so used, and
        (ii) as used as a feeding stuff whether it is so used by itself, or as an ingredient in something which is to be so used.
    (c) paragraph (b) shall not apply in any circumstances in which Article 16 (labelling and packaging of feed additives and premixtures) of Regulation (EC) No. 1831/2003 of the European Parliament and of the Council on additives for use in animal nutrition applies.(a)".

(3) Sections 73 and 73A shall have effect in England as if, for the words "animals of any description prescribed for the purpose of the definition of "feeding stuff" in section 66(1) of this Act" there were substituted the words "any farmed creatures".

(4) Section 85 shall have effect in England as if—
    (a) in so far as it relates to delivery outside the United Kingdom, paragraph (a) were omitted; and
    (b) paragraph (b) were omitted.

Modification of the Agriculture Act 1970 in relation to imported feeding stuffs

4. In relation to feeding stuffs which have been imported, section 69(1) shall have effect in England as if the words "and in either case before it is removed from the premises" were omitted.

Prescribed material to which requirements for the statutory statement and marking apply

5.—(1) Subject to paragraph (2), the material prescribed for the purposes of sections 68(1) and 69(1) is any material usable as a feeding stuff.

(2) For the purposes of these Regulations section 68(2) does not apply.

(a) OJ No. L268, 18.10.2003, p. 29.

Exemption from these Regulations

6. In so far as provisions of these Regulations implement the Compound Feedingstuffs Directive (which principally regulates the labelling and packaging of compound feeding stuffs), they shall not apply in the circumstances specified in Article 14(c) (relating to animals kept for scientific or experimental purposes) of that Directive.

Revocations

7. The Feeding Stuffs Regulations 2000, with the exception of regulation 19A and paragraph 19 of Schedule 4 of those Regulations, are revoked in relation to England, together with the amending instruments listed in Schedule 9 and to the extent specified in that Schedule.

PART 2

Presentation and Composition of Feeding Stuffs

Matters required and permitted to be contained in a statutory statement or otherwise declared

8. Except in respect of additives and premixtures not contained in feeding stuffs, the particulars, information and instructions required or permitted to be contained in a statutory statement or otherwise declared, are as specified in and shall comply with the provisions of Schedule 3.

Forms of statutory statement

9.—(1) Except in the circumstances relating to small quantities of feeding stuffs mentioned in Article 5(2) of the Compound Feedingstuffs Directive and subject to paragraph (2), the statutory statement—

    (a) in the case of any prescribed material delivered in a package or other container, shall—

        (i) take the form of a label attached to that package or container; or

        (ii) be clearly marked directly on the package or container, and

    (b) in the case of such material delivered in bulk, shall take the form of a document relating to and accompanying each consignment.

(2) In the case of any feed material sold in a quantity not exceeding 10 kg, and supplied directly to the final user, the statutory statement may be provided in the form of a notice in writing.

(3) The particulars, information and instructions required or permitted to be contained in the statutory statement shall—

    (a) be clearly separate from any other information;

    (b) subject to paragraphs (5) and (6), be in English; and

    (c) be legible and indelible.

(4) For the purposes of section 69 (marking of material prepared for sale), prescribed material which is contained in a package or other container shall be labelled or marked in the manner prescribed in relation to such material in paragraph (1)(a) or, where applicable, (2), and such material in bulk shall be marked by the display in as close proximity to the material as may be practicable of a document relating thereto.

(5) In the case of any compound feeding stuff or feed material which is intended for export to a Member State, the statutory statement shall be in one or more official Community languages, as determined by that Member State.

(6) In the case of any feeding stuff, except a feeding stuff containing an additive in category (d) or (e) of Article 6(1) of the Additives Regulation other than those in the functional groups listed in paragraph 4(a), (b) or (c) of Annex 1 to that Regulation, which is intended for export to an EEA State that is not a Member State, the statutory statement shall be in one or more of the official languages of the country of destination.

Limits of variation

10.—(1) Section 74(2) shall have effect in England as if after the words "this Part of this Act" there were inserted the words "or the Feeding Stuffs (England) Regulations 2005".

(2) For the purposes of section 74, as modified by paragraph (1), the limits of variation in relation to any mis-statement in a statutory statement, document or mark, as to the nature, substance or quality of a feeding stuff where the mis-statement relates to—

    (a) any analytical constituent specified in the first column of—

        (i) Part A of Schedule 4 (where the feeding stuff is a compound feeding stuff not intended for pet animals),

        (ii) Part B of Schedule 4 (where the feeding stuff is a compound pet food), or

        (iii) Part C of Schedule 4 (in the case of a feed material);

    (b) any vitamin or trace element specified in the first column of Part D of that Schedule; or

    (c) the energy value of any feeding stuff specified in the first column of Part E of that Schedule,

shall be as set out with respect to that constituent or vitamin, trace element or feeding stuff, in the corresponding entry in the second Column of the relevant Part of that Schedule.

(3) Particulars with respect to any material which are contained in a statutory statement, or in any document, or which are marked on, or denoted by a mark on, the material, shall not, for the purposes of Part IV of the Act or of these Regulations, be treated as false by reason of any mis-statement therein as to the nature, substance or quality of the material, if—

    (a) the material was first sold, or otherwise put into circulation in an EEA State;

    (b) the mis-statement did not, at the time of putting into circulation, exceed any limits of variation prescribed in relation thereto in the State concerned; and

    (c) any such limits were in accordance with any applicable European Community legislation.

Assigned meanings for statutory statements or marks

11. For the purposes of section 70, there is assigned to the expressions "complementary feeding stuff", "complete feeding stuff", "compound feeding stuff", "milk replacer feed", "mineral feeding stuff" and "molassed feeding stuff" in each case the meaning given by regulation 2(1) to the expression concerned.

Manner of packaging and sealing compound feeding stuffs

12.—(1) Subject to paragraphs (2) and (3), no person shall put into circulation a compound feeding stuff, unless it is in a bag or container, and that bag or container is sealed in such a way that, when the bag or container is opened, the seal is damaged and cannot be re-used.

(2) Compound feeding stuffs may be put into circulation in bulk, in unsealed bags or in unsealed containers, in the case of—

    (a) deliveries between producers of compound feeding stuffs or those putting them into circulation;

    (b) deliveries from producers of compound feeding stuffs to packaging enterprises;

    (c) compound feeding stuffs obtained by mixing grain or whole fruit;

    (d) blocks or licks;

    (e) small quantities not exceeding 50 kg in weight, which are intended for the final user and are taken directly from a bag or container which, before opening, complied with the sealing provision in paragraph (1).

(3) Compound feeding stuffs may be put into circulation in bulk, or in unsealed containers, but not in unsealed bags, in the case of—

    (a) direct deliveries from the producer to the final user;

    (b) molassed feeding stuffs consisting of less than three feed materials;

    (c) pelleted feeding stuffs.

Control of feed materials

13.—(1) In this regulation any reference to a numbered Part means a Part of Schedule 2.

(2) No person shall put into circulation any feed material of a description specified in column (3) of Part II under a name other than that specified in the corresponding entry in column (2) of that Part.

(3) No person shall put into circulation any feed material not listed in Part II under a name specified in column (2) of that Part or under a name or term which could otherwise mislead a purchaser as to the real identity of the material.

(4) Where the name of a feed material listed in column (2) of Part II includes a common name or term listed in column (4) of Part I no person shall put into circulation any such feed material or any compound feeding stuff containing such feed material unless the feed material was prepared by the process specified in columns (2) and (3) of Part I corresponding to that common name or term.

(5) No person shall put into circulation any feed material or any compound feeding stuff containing any feed material, unless—

(a) in the case of any feed material of a description specified in column (3) of Part II the botanical purity by weight of the feed material is not less than the percentage (if any) specified in relation to it in column (3) of Part II or, if none is specified, is not less than 95%; or

(b) in the case of any feed material of a description specified in column (1) of Part III the botanical purity by weight of the feed material is not less than 95%; and

the feed material also complies with the provisions regarding botanical and chemical purity set out in paragraph 1 of Section II of Part A of the Annex to the Feed Materials Directive.

(6) No person shall use any feed material to bind another feed material, if the quantity of the feed material so used exceeds 3% of the total weight of the feed material bound.

(7) Without prejudice to sections 73 and 73A, no person shall import into England from any state which is not an EEA State, supply (otherwise than on sale), have in possession with a view to so supplying or use any feed material which is deleterious or dangerous to farmed creatures, to pet animals or, through consumption of the products of any animal fed with the feed material, to human beings.

(8) No person shall put into circulation or use any feed material which presents a danger to the environment.

(9) No person shall put into circulation any feed material in a manner likely to mislead as to its properties.

(10) In paragraph (5)(a) "description" shall be taken to exclude any botanical purity requirement, and for the purposes of this regulation and of Schedule 2 "botanical purity" shall be construed in accordance with paragraph 2 of Section II of Part A of the Annex to the Feed Materials Directive.

Control of products intended for animal feed containing undesirable substances

14.—(1) No person shall—

(a) put into circulation any product intended for animal feed which is specified in column 2 of Schedule 5; or

(b) use any such product for animal feed,

if it contains any undesirable substance specified in column 1 of that Schedule in excess of the level specified for it in column 3 of that Schedule.

(2) No person shall put into circulation, or use as a feeding stuff, any complementary feeding stuff if—

(a) having regard to the quantity of it recommended for use in a daily ration, it contains any undesirable substance specified in column 1 of Schedule 5 in excess of the level specified for it in column 3 of that Schedule in relation to complete feeding stuffs; and

(b) there is no provision relating to any complementary feeding stuff in the corresponding entry in column 2 of that Schedule.

(3) No person shall mix any product intended for animal feed which is specified in column 2 of Schedule 5 and which contains any undesirable substance specified in column 1 of that Schedule in excess of the level specified for it in column 3 of that Schedule for the purpose of dilution with any product intended for animal feed.

(4) No person shall put into circulation any product intended for animal feed or use any such product for animal feed unless it is—

(a) sound and genuine; and

(b) of merchantable quality.

(5) For the purposes of paragraph (4), a product intended for animal feed which is specified in column 2 of Schedule 5 is not sound, genuine and of merchantable quality if it contains any undesirable substance specified in column 1 of that Schedule in excess of the level specified in relation to it in column 3 of that Schedule.

(6) For the purposes of paragraph (2) "feeding stuff" includes feeding stuffs for oral feeding to animals living freely in the wild, and "complementary feeding stuff" and "complete feeding stuff" shall be construed accordingly.

(7) Paragraph (8) shall apply to any person who has in his possession or control for the purpose of a trade or business any of the following products intended for animal feed—

(a) palm kernel expeller;

(b) feeding stuffs obtained from the processing of fish or other marine animals;

(c) seaweed meal and feed materials derived from seaweed; or

(d) complete feeding stuffs for fish or for fur producing animals.

(8) Any person referred to in paragraph (7) shall, if requested by an inspector, procure and produce to the inspector an analysis in order to demonstrate that the content of inorganic arsenic in a product intended for animal feed listed in paragraph (7) is within the limit specified in the relevant entry in column 3 of Schedule 5.

(9) Any person who without reasonable excuse fails to comply with a request made under paragraph (8) shall be guilty of an offence and liable on summary conviction to a fine not exceeding level 3 on the standard scale.

Control of feeding stuffs containing prohibited materials

15.—(1) No person shall put into circulation for use as a feeding stuff, or use as a feeding stuff, any material which contains—

(a) faeces, urine or separated digestive tract contents resulting from the emptying or removal of the digestive tract, irrespective of any form of treatment or admixture;

(b) hide treated with tanning substances, including its waste;

(c) seeds or other plant propagating materials which, after harvest, have undergone specific treatment with plant protection products for their intended propagation, or derived by-products;

(d) wood, sawdust or other materials derived from wood which has been treated with wood preservatives as defined in Annex V to Directive 98/8/EC of the European Parliament and of the Council concerning the placing of biocidal products on the market(a);

(e) subject to paragraph (3), waste (whether or not subjected, or to be subjected, to further processing) obtained from the treatment of "urban waste water", "domestic waste water" or "industrial waste water" (as those terms are defined in Article 2 of Council Directive 91/271/EEC concerning urban waste water treatment), whatever the origin of the waste water concerned(b);

(a) OJ No. L123, 24.4.98, p. 1, as amended by Regulation (EC) 1882/2003 of the European Parliament and of the Council (OJ No. L284, 31.10.2003, p. 1).

(b) OJ No. L135, 30.5.1991, p. 40, as last amended by Regulation (EC) 1882/2003 of the European Parliament and of the Council (OJ No. L284, 31.10.2003, p. 1).

(f) solid urban waste, such as household waste, but excluding catering waste as defined by Regulation (EC) 1774/2002 of the European Parliament and of the Council laying down health rules concerning animal by-products not intended for human consumption(**a**);

(g) packaging and parts of packaging from products used in agriculture or the food industry.

(2) For the purposes of paragraph (1) "waste" has the meaning given in Article 1 of Council Directive 75/442/EEC on waste(**b**).

(3) For the purposes of paragraph 1(e), the term "waste water" shall be construed in accordance with the footnote to point 5 of the Annex to Commission Decision 2004/217/EC establishing a list of materials whose circulation or use for animal nutrition purposes is prohibited(**c**).

Control of certain protein sources

16.—(1) Subject to paragraphs (3) and (4), no person shall sell or have in possession with a view to sale, for use as a feeding stuff or as a protein source in a feeding stuff, any material belonging to a product group specified in column 1 of Schedule 6, unless that material—

(a) is named as a permitted product in column 2 of that Schedule; and

(b) complies with all the specifications and requirements contained in and imposed in relation thereto by columns 3 to 6 of that Schedule.

(2) Subject to paragraph (3), no person shall sell or have in possession with a view to sale for use as a feeding stuff, or use as a feeding stuff, any product obtained from yeasts of the "Candida" variety cultivated on n-alkanes.

(3) Paragraphs (1) and (2) do not apply in relation to any material or product excluded from application of the Certain Products Directive by Article 16 thereof concerning exports to third countries.

(4) Paragraph (1) does not apply in the circumstances authorised for derogation by Article 3(2) (concerning scientific or experimental purposes) of the Certain Products Directive.

Control of the iron content of milk replacer feeds

17. No person shall put into circulation any milk replacer feed intended for calves of up to 70 kilograms live weight, which has an iron content of less than 30 milligrams per kilogram of the complete feeding stuff at a moisture content of 12%.

Control of ash insoluble in hydrochloric acid in compound feeding stuffs

18.—(1) No person shall put into circulation—

(a) any compound feeding stuff composed mainly of rice by-products in which the level of ash insoluble in hydrochloric acid exceeds 3.3% of its dry matter; or

(b) subject to paragraph (2), any other compound feeding stuff in which the level of ash insoluble in hydrochloric acid exceeds 2.2% of its dry matter.

(2) Paragraph (1)(b) shall not apply to the putting into circulation of any compound feeding stuff which—

(a) contains permitted mineral binders named or described in the Annex to Commission Directive 2003/57/EC(**d**);

(b) is a mineral feeding stuff;

(**a**) OJ No. L273, 10.10.2002, p. 1, as amended by Commission Regulation (EC) 808/2003 (OJ No. L117, 13.5.2003, p. 1).
(**b**) OJ No. L194, 25.7.95, p. 39, as last amended by Regulation (EC) No. 1882/2003 of the European Parliament and of the Council (OJ No. L284, 31.10.2003, p. 1).
(**c**) OJ No. L67, 5.3.2004, p. 31.
(**d**) OJ No. L151, 19.6.2003, p. 38, amending Directive 2002/32/EC of the European Parliament and of the Council on undesirable substances in animal feed (OJ No. L140, 30.5.2002, p. 10).

(c) contains more than 50% of sugar beet chips or sugar beet pulp; or

(d) is intended for farmed fish and has a fish meal content of more than 15%,

if the level of ash insoluble in hydrochloric acid is declared in the statutory statement as a percentage of the feeding stuff as such.

Control of feeding stuffs intended for particular nutritional purposes, and supplementary provisions relating to statutory statement

19.—(1) No person shall put into circulation any feeding stuff intended for a particular nutritional purpose unless—

(a) the particular nutritional purpose in question is specified in column 1 of Chapter A of Schedule 7;

(b) the feeding stuff possesses the essential nutritional characteristics specified opposite that particular nutritional purpose in column 2 of that Chapter;

(c) the feeding stuff is intended for animals specified opposite that particular nutritional purpose in column 3 of that Chapter;

(d) it is recommended that the feeding stuff be used for a period of time falling within the range specified opposite that particular nutritional purpose in column 5 of that Chapter;

(e) in relation to the feeding stuff, the requirements specified in paragraphs 1, 2 and 8 of Chapter B of Schedule 7 are complied with; and

(f) the composition of the feeding stuff is such that it is capable of achieving the particular nutritional purpose for which it is intended.

(2) Schedule 7 shall have effect as specified in Schedule 3.

Control of additives and premixtures

20.—(1) No person shall contravene or fail to comply with the provisions of the Additives Regulation specified in paragraph (2).

(2) The provisions referred to in paragraph (1) are—

(a) Article 3 (placing on the market, processing and use of feed additives), paragraphs (1) to (4), as read with Article 10 (status of existing products);

(b) Article 12 (supervision);

(c) Article 16, paragraphs (1) to (5), (labelling and packaging of additives and premixtures).

(3) In any proceedings for an offence under paragraph (2)(a) it shall be a defence to prove that the act giving rise to the offence—

(a) is one to which Article 10 of the Additives Regulation applies; and

(b) would not have constituted an offence under the 2000 Regulations as they were immediately before the coming into force of these Regulations.

(4) In any proceedings for an offence under paragraph (2)(c) it shall be a defence to prove that the act giving rise to the offence—

(a) is one to which Article 25(2) of the Additives Regulation applies; and

(b) would not have constituted an offence under the 2000 Regulations as they were immediately before the coming into force of these Regulations.

(5) Notwithstanding the revocation referred to in regulation 7, where before the 18th October 2004 initial comments had been forwarded to the Commission in accordance with regulation 11(2) of the 2000 Regulations that application shall be treated as if regulation 11 of those Regulations were still in force.

Saving relating to confidential information relating to additives under the 2000 Regulations

21.—(1) Notwithstanding the revocations in regulation 7, and subject to paragraphs (2) and (3), no person shall publish or disclose any confidential information that was, prior to the coming into force of these Regulations, obtained by him in the performance of functions under regulation 11 of the 2000 Regulations without the previous consent in writing of—

    (a) the person who, in accordance with that regulation, made an application for a Community authorisation of, or as the case may be, for a new use of, the additive concerned; or

    (b) that person's assignee or successor to ownership of the confidential information.

(2) Nothing in paragraph (1) shall restrict the publication or disclosure of such information for the purpose of the exercise of functions under that regulation.

(3) Nothing in paragraph (1) shall prevent the publication or disclosure of confidential information of a type specified in Article 7(2) of the Additives Directive.

(4) In this regulation, "confidential information" means information of the type specified in Article 7(1) of the Additives Directive and "additive" has the meaning given in Article 2 of that Directive.

(5) A publication or disclosure in contravention of paragraph (1) shall be punishable as if it were a disclosure prohibited by section 83.

PART 3

Enforcement

Enforcement of provisions made under section 2(2) of the European Communities Act 1972

22. In so far as any provision of these Regulations is made under section 2(2) of the European Communities Act 1972, that provision shall be enforced as if it were made under those provisions of Part IV of the Act under which the other provisions of these Regulations are made, and the provisions of that Part shall apply accordingly.

Modification of section 74A(3) of the Agriculture Act 1970

23.—(1) For the purposes of the enforcement and administration of the provisions specified in paragraph (2), section 74A(3) shall have effect as if for the words "imposed by regulations under subsection (1) above, or fails to comply with any other provision of the regulations," there were substituted the words "or fails to comply with any requirement imposed by any provision specified in regulation 23(2) of the Feeding Stuffs (England) Regulations 2005".

(2) The provisions specified for the purposes of paragraph (1) are regulation 12(1), 13(2) to (9), 14(1) to (4), 15(1), 16(1) and (2), 17, 18(1), 19(1) and 20(1).

PART 4

Amendments to other legislation

Amendments to the Feeding Stuffs (Sampling and Analysis) Regulations 1999

24.—(1) The Feeding Stuffs (Sampling and Analysis) Regulations 1999(**a**) are amended in relation to England in accordance with paragraphs (2) to (4).

(2) In Schedule 2 Part I (general provisions), in sub-paragraph 3(e)(ii) for the words "listed in Schedule 7" to the end of the sub-paragraph substitute the expression "listed in Schedule 5 to the Feeding Stuffs (England) Regulations 2005".

(3) In Annex 1 to Part II of Schedule 2 for the second entry for Starch (polarimetric method) substitute—

    (a) in column 2 the words "Point 1 of Annex 1 to Directive 72/1999/EEC (as replaced entirely by the Annex to Directive 1999/79/EC)";

    (b) in column 3 the words "OJ No. L123, 29.5.72, p. 6 (OJ/SE 1966-1972 supplement p. 74) OJ No. L209, 7.8.99, p. 23".

(**a**) S.I. 1999/1663. These Regulations are subject to a number of amendments but none is relevant.

(4) In Schedule 3 Part II (notes for completion of certificate), in sub-paragraph (a) of note (11)—

   (a) omit the expression "as amended" through to and including the expression "Feeding Stuffs (Enforcement) (Amendment) (England) (No. 2) Regulations 2003";

   (b) for the expression "Feeding Stuffs Regulations 2000" substitute "Feeding Stuffs (England) Regulations 2005".

Signed by authority of the Secretary of State for Health

Caroline Flint
Parliamentary Under Secretary of State,
28th November 2005   Department of Health

14

METHOD OF CALCULATING THE ENERGY VALUE OF COMPOUND FEEDS

The energy value of compound poultry, ruminant and pig feeds and feeding stuffs intended for particular nutritional purposes for cats and dogs shall be calculated in accordance with the relevant formulae set out below, on the basis of the percentages of certain analytical components of the feed. After application of these formulae, the results shall be given to one decimal place.

Poultry feeds: megajoules (MJ) of metabolisable energy (ME), nitrogen corrected, per kilogram of compound feed.

MJ of ME/kg of feed = 0.1551 × % protein[1] + 0.3431 × % oil[2] + 0.1669 × % starch[3] + 0.1301 × % total sugar (expressed as sucrose)[4].

Ruminant feeds: megajoules (MJ) of metabolisable energy (ME) per kilogram of dry matter in the compound feed.

MJ of ME/kg of dry matter = 0.14 × % Neutral detergent Cellulase plus Gamanase Digestibility[5] + 0.25 × % oil[2].

Pig feeds: megajoules (MJ) of digestible energy (DE) per kilogram of dry matter in the compound feed.

MJ of DE/kg of dry matter = 17.47 + 0.079 × % protein[1] + 0.158 × % oil[2] − 0.331 × % ash[6] − 0.140 Neutral Detergent plus Amylase Fibre[5].

[NB] Where the results of analysis are to be given on a dry matter basis, this may be achieved by analysing either the dried material, or fresh material and correcting for the moisture content.

[1] Determined by the method of analysis for protein specified in Point 2 of Annex 1 to Directive 72/199/EC(**a**).

[NB] For pig feed the results must be corrected to 100% dry matter.

[2] Determined by the appropriate procedure set out in the method of analysis for oils and fats specified in Part IV of the Annex to Directive 71/393/EEC(**b**).

[NB] In ruminant and pig feeds the result must be corrected to 100% dry matter.

[3] Determined by the method of analysis for starch specified in Point 1 of Annex 1 to Directive 72/199/EEC(**c**).

[4] Determined by the method of analysis for sugar specified in Point 12 of the Annex to Directive 71/250/EEC(**d**).

[5] Determined by the method detailed in the booklet "Prediction of Energy Values of Compound Feeding Stuffs for Farm Animals" (originally published by the Ministry of Agriculture, Fisheries and Food Publications, now available from the Department of the Environment, Food and Rural Affairs under reference No. PB1285).

[6] Determined by the method of analysis for ash specified in Point 5 of the Annex to Directive 71/250/EEC(**e**).

[NB] The result must be corrected to 100% dry matter.

(**a**) OJ No. L123, 29.5.72, p. 6 (OJ/SE 1966–1972 supplement, p. 74). Point 2 of Annex 1 has been replaced entirely by the Annex to Directive 93/28/EC (OJ No. L179, 22.7.93, p. 8).

(**b**) OJ No. L279, 20.12.71, p. 7 (OJ/SE 1971(III), p. 987). Part IV was entirely replaced by Annex 1 to Directive 84/4/EEC (OJ No. L15, 18.1.84, p. 28). That Annex was in turn replaced entirely by Part B of the Annex to Directive 98/64/EC (OJ No. L257, 19.9.98, p. 14).

(**c**) OJ No. L123, 29.5.72, p. 6 (OJ/SE 1966-1972 supplement, p. 74) (as replaced entirely by the Annex to Directive 1999/79/EC (OJ No. L209, 7.8.1999, p. 23)).

(**d**) OJ No. L155, 12.7.71, p. 13 (OJ/SE 1971(II), p. 480) as corrected by a corrigendum published in July 1975 (consolidated edition of corrigenda to the first series of specified editions of EC legislation (1952 to 1972)).

(**e**) OJ No. L155, 12.7.71, p. 13 (OJ/SE 1971(II), p. 480).

CONTROL OF FEED MATERIALS

PART I

PRINCIPAL PROCESSES USED FOR THE PREPARATION OF THE FEED MATERIALS LISTED IN PART II OF THIS SCHEDULE

	Process (1)	Definition (2)	Common name or term (3)
1	Concentration[1]	Increase in certain contents by removing water or other constituents	Concentrate
2	Decortication[2]	Complete or partial removal of outer layers from grains, seeds, fruits nuts and others	Decorticated, partially decorticated
3	Drying	Dehydration by artificial or natural processes	Dried (sun or artificially)
4	Extraction	Removal either by organic solvent of fat or oil from certain materials or by aqueous solvent of sugar or other water–soluble components. In the case of the use of organic solvent, the resulting product must be technically free of such solvent	Extracted (in the case of oil-containing materials), molasses, pulp (in the case of products containing sugar or other water–soluble components)
5	Extrusion	Pressing of material through an orifice under pressure. (See also pregelatinisation)	Extruded
6	Flaking	Rolling of moist heat-treated material	Flakes
7	Flour milling	Physical processing of grain to reduce particle size and facilitate separation into constituent fractions (principally flour, bran and middlings)	Flour, bran, middlings[3], feed
8	Heating	General term covering a number of heat treatments carried out under specific conditions to influence the nutritional value or the structure of the material	Toasted, cooked, heat treated
9	Hydrogenation	Transformation of unsaturated glycerides into saturated glycerides (of oils and fats)	Hardened, partially hardened
10	Hydrolysis	Breakdown into simpler chemical constituents by appropriate treatment with water and possibly either enzymes or acid/alkali	Hydrolysed
11	Pressing[4]	Removal by mechanical extraction (by a screw or other type of press), with or without a slight heating, of fat/oil from oil–rich materials or of juice from fruits or other vegetable products	Expeller[5] (in case of oil–containing materials) Pulp, pomace (in case of fruits, etc.) Pressed pulp (in case of sugar-beet)
12	Pelleting	Special shaping by compression through a die	Pellet, pelleted
13	Pregelatinisation	Modification of starch to improve markedly its swelling properties in cold water	Pregelatinised[6], puffed

14	Refining	Complete or partial removal of impurities in sugars, oils, fats and other natural materials by chemical/physical treatment	Refined, partially refined
15	Wet–milling	Mechanical separation of the component parts of kernel/grain, sometimes after steeping in water, with or without sulphur dioxide, for the extraction of starch	Germ, gluten, starch
16	Crushing	Mechanical processing of grain or other feed materials to reduce their size	Crushed, crushing
17	Desugaring	Complete or partial removal of mono– and disaccharides from molasses and other material containing sugar by chemical or physical means	Desugared, partially desugared

[1] In German 'Konzentrieren' may be replaced by 'Eindicken' where appropriate, in which case the common qualifier should be 'eingedickt'.

[2] Decortication' may be replaced by 'dehulling' or 'dehusking' where appropriate, in which case the common qualifier should be 'dehulled' or 'dehusked.'

[3] In French the name 'issues' may be used.

[4] In French 'Pressage' may be replaced by 'Exraction mécanique' where appropriate.

[5] Where appropriate the word 'expeller' may be replaced by 'cake'.

[6] In German the qualifier 'aufgeschlossen' and the name 'Quellwasser' (referring to starch) may be used

PART II
NON-EXCLUSIVE LIST OF THE MAIN FEED MATERIALS

Introductory Notes

Feed materials are listed and named in this Part according to the following criteria:

– the origin of the product/by–product used, for example vegetable, animal, mineral,

– the part of the product/by–product used, for example whole, seeds, tubers, bones,

– the processing to which the product/by–product has been subjected, for example decortication, extraction, heating and/or the resulting product/by–product, for example flakes, bran, pulp, fat,

– the maturity of the product/by–product and/or the quality of the product/by–product, for example 'low in glocosinolate', 'rich in fat', 'low in sugar'.

Number (1)	Name (2)	Description (3)	Compulsory declarations (4)
1. Cereal, grains, their products and by–products			
1.01	Oats	Grains of *Avena sativa* L. and other cultivars of oats.	
1.02	Oat flakes	Product obtained by steaming and rolling dehusked oats. It may contain a small proportion of oat husks.	Starch
1.03	Oat middlings	By–product obtained during the processing of screened, dehusked oats into oat groats and flour. It consists principally of oat bran and some endosperm.	Fibre
1.04	Oat hulls and bran	By–product obtained during the processing of screened oats into oat groats. It consists principally of oat hulls and bran.	Fibre
1.05	Barley	Grains of *Hordeum vulgare* L.	
1.06	Barley middlings	By–product obtained during the processing of screened, dehusked barley into pearl barley, semolina or flour.	Fibre
1.07	Barley protein	Dried by–product of starch production from barley. It consists principally of protein obtained from starch separation.	Protein Starch

Number (1)	Name (2)	Description (3)	Compulsory declarations (4)
1.08	Rice, broken	By–product of preparation of polished or glazed rice *Oryza sativa* L. It consists principally of undersized and/or broken grains.	Starch
1.09	Rice bran (brown)	By–product of the first polishing of dehusked rice. It consists principally of particles of the aleurone layer, endosperm and germ.	Fibre
1.10	Rice bran (white)	By–product of the polishing of dehusked rice. It consists principally of particles of the aleurone layer, endosperm and germ.	Fibre
1.11	Rice bran with calcium carbonate	By–product of the polishing of dehusked rice. It consists principally of silvery skins, particles of the aleurone layer, endosperm and germ; it contains varying amounts of calcium carbonate resulting from the polishing process.	Fibre Calcium carbonate
1.12	Fodder meal of parboiled rice	By–product of the polishing of dehusked pre-cooked rice. It consists principally of silvery skins, particles of the aleurone layer, endosperm and germ; it contains varying amounts of calcium carbonate resulting from the polishing process.	Fibre Calcium carbonate
1.13	Ground fodder rice	Product obtained by grinding fodder rice, consisting either of green, chalky or unripe grains, sifted out during the milling of husked rice, or of normal dehusked grains which are yellow or spotted.	Starch
1.14	Rice germ expeller	By–product of oil manufacture, obtained by pressing of the germ of rice to which parts of the endosperm and testa still adhere.	Protein Fat Fibre
1.15	Rice germ, extracted	By–product of oil manufacture obtained by extraction of the germ of rice to which parts of the endosperm and testa still adhere.	Protein
1.16	Rice starch	Technically pure rice starch.	Starch
1.17	Millet	Grains of *Panicum miliaceum* L.	
1.18	Rye	Grains of *Secale cereale* L.	
1.19	Rye Middlings[1]	By–product of flour manufacture, obtained from screened rye. It consists principally of particles of endosperm, with fine fragments of the outer skins and some grain waste.	Starch
1.20	Rye feed	By–product of flour manufacture, obtained from screened rye. It consists principally of fragments of the outer skins, and of particles of grain from which less of the endosperm has been removed than in rye bran.	Starch
1.21	Rye bran	By–product of flour manufacture, obtained from screened rye. It consists principally of fragments of the outer skins, and of particles of grain from which most of the endosperm has been removed.	Fibre
1.22	Sorghum	Grains of *Sorghum bicolor* (L.) *Moench s.l.*	
1.23	Wheat	Grains of *Triticum aestivum* (L.), *Triticum durum* Desf. and other cultivars of wheat.	
1.24	Wheat middlings[2]	By–product of flour manufacture, obtained from screened grains of wheat or dehusked spelt. It consists principally of particles of endosperm with fine fragments of the outer skins and some grain waste.	Starch

Number (1)	Name (2)	Description (3)	Compulsory declarations (4)
1.25	Wheat feed	By–product of flour manufacture, obtained from screened grains of wheat or dehusked spelt. It consists principally of fragments of the outer skins and of particles of grain from which less of the endosperm has been removed than in wheat bran.	Fibre
1.26	Wheat Bran[3]	By–product of flour manufacture, obtained from screened grains of wheat or dehusked spelt. It consists principally of fragments of the outer skins and of particles of grain from which the greater part of the endosperm has been removed.	Fibre
1.27	Wheat germ	By–product of flour milling consisting essentially of wheat germ, rolled or otherwise, to which fragments of endosperm and outer skin may still adhere.	Protein Fat
1.28	Wheat gluten	Dried by–product of the manufacture of wheat starch. It consists principally of gluten obtained during the separation of starch.	Protein
1.29	Wheat gluten feed	By–product of the manufacture of wheat starch and gluten. It is composed of bran, from which the germ has been partially removed or not, and gluten, to which very small amounts of the components of the screening of the grain as well as very small amount of residues of the starch hydrolysis process may be added.	Protein Starch
1.30	Wheat starch	Technically pure starch obtained from wheat.	Starch
1.31	Pre–gelatinised wheat starch	Product consisting of wheat starch largely expanded by heat treatment.	Starch
1.32	Spelt	Grains of spelt *Triticum spelta L., Tricicum dioccum Schrank, Triticum monococcum*.	
1.33	Triticale	Grains of *Triticum X secale* hybrid.	
1.34	Maize	Grains of *Zea mays* L.	
1.35	Maize middlings[4]	By–product of the manufacture of flour or semolina from maize. It consists principally of fragments of the outer skins and of particles of grain from which less of the endosperm has been removed than in maize bran.	Fibre
1.36	Maize bran	By–product of the manufacture of flour or semolina from maize. It consists principally of outer skins and some maize germ fragments, with some endosperm particles.	Fibre
1.37	Maize germ expeller	By–product of oil manufacture, obtained by pressing of dry or wet processed maize germ to which parts of the endosperm and testa may still adhere.	Protein Fat
1.38	Maize germ, extracted	By–product of oil manufacture, obtained by extraction of dry or wet processed maize germ to which parts of the endosperm and testa may still adhere.	Protein
1.39	Maize gluten feed[5]	By–product of the wet manufacture of maize starch. It is composed of bran and gluten, to which the broken maize obtained from screening at an amount no greater than 15% of the product and/or the residues of the steeping liquor used for the production of alcohol or other starch-derived products, may be added. The product may also include residues from the oil extraction of maize germs obtained also by a wet process.	Protein Starch Fat, if > 4.5%
1.40	Maize gluten	Dried by–product of the manufacture of maize starch. It consists principally of gluten obtained during the separation of the starch.	Protein

Number (1)	Name (2)	Description (3)	Compulsory declarations (4)
1.41	Maize starch	Technically pure starch obtained from maize	Starch
1.42	Pre-gelatinised maize starch[6]	Product consisting of maize starch largely expanded by heat treatment.	Starch
1.43	Malt culms	By-product of malting, consisting mainly of dried rootlets of germinated cereals.	Protein
1.44	Brewers' dried grains	By-product of brewing obtained by drying residues of malted and unmalted cereals and other starchy products.	Protein
1.45	Distiller's dried grains[7]	By-product of alcohol distilling obtained by drying solid residues of fermented grain.	Protein
1.46	Distiller's dark grains[8]	By-product of alcohol distilling obtained by drying solid residues of fermented grain to which pot ale syrup or evaporated spent wash has been added.	Protein

[1] Products containing more than 40% starch may be qualified as 'rich in starch'. They may be referred to in German as 'Roggennachmehl'.

[2] Products containing more than 40% starch may be qualified as 'rich in starch'. They may be referred to in German as 'Weizennachmehl'.

[3] If this ingredient has been subjected to a finer milling the word 'fine' may be added to the name or the name may be replaced by a corresponding denomination.

[4] Products containing more than 40% starch may be named as 'rich in starch'. They may be referred to in German as 'Maisnachmehl'.

[5] This name may be replaced by 'corn gluten feed'.

[6] This name may be replaced by 'extruded maize starch'.

[7] The name may be supplemented by the grain species.

[8] This name may be replaced by 'distillers' dried grains and solubles'. The name may be supplemented by the grain species.

2. Oil seeds, oil fruits, their products and by-products

2.01	Groundnut, partially decorticated, expeller	By-product of oil manufacture, obtained by pressing of partially decorticated groundnuts Arachis hypogaea L. and other species of Arachis. (Maximum fibre content 16% in the dry matter)	Protein Fat Fibre
2.02	Groundnut, partially decorticated, extracted	By-product of oil manufacture obtained by extraction of partially decorticated grounds. (Maximum fibre content 16% in the dry matter)	Protein Fibre
2.03	Groundnut, decorticated, expeller	By-product of oil manufacture, obtained by pressing of decorticated groundnuts	Protein Fat Fibre
2.04	Groundnut, decorticated, extracted	By-product of oil manufacture, obtained by extraction of decorticated grounds	Protein Fibre
2.05	Rape seed[1]	Seeds of rape Brassica napus L. ssp. oleifera (Metzg.) Sinsk., of Indian sarson Brassica napus L. Var. Glauca (Roxb.) O.E. Schulz and of rape Brassica napa ssp. oleifera (Metzg). Sinsk. (Minimum botanical purity 94%).	
2.06	Rape seed, expeller[1]	By-product of oil manufacture, obtained by extraction of seeds of rape. (Minimum botanical purity 94%).	Protein Fat Fibre
2.07	Rape seed, extracted[1]	By-product of oil manufacture, obtained by extraction of seeds of rape. (Minimum botanical purity 94%)	Protein

2.08	Rape seed hulls	By–product obtained during dehulling of rape seeds	Fibre
2.09	Safflower seed, partially decorticated, extracted	By–product of oil manufacture, obtained by extraction of partially decorticated seeds of safflower *Carthamus tinctorius* L.	Protein Fibre
2.10	Copra expeller	By–product of oil manufacture, obtained by pressing the dried kernel (endosperm) and outer husk (tegument) of the seed of the coconut palm *Cocos nucifera* L.	Protein Fat Fibre
2.11	Copra, extracted	By–product of oil manufacture, obtained by extraction of the dried kernel (endosperm) and outer husk (tegument) of the seed of the coconut palm.	Protein
2.12	Palm kernel expeller	By–product of oil manufacture, obtained by pressing of palm kernels *Elaeis guineensis* Jacq. *Corozo oleifera* (HBK) L. H. Bailey *(Elaeis melanocca auct.)* from which as much as possible of the hard shell has been removed.	Protein Fibre Fat
2.13	Palm kernel, extracted	By–product of oil manufacture, obtained by extraction of palm kernels from which as much as possible of the hard shell has been removed.	Protein Fibre
2.14	Soya (bean), toasted	Soya beans (*Glycine max.* L. Merr.) subjected to an appropriate heat treatment. (Urease activity maximum 0.4 mg N/g x min.)	
2.15	Soya (bean), extracted, toasted	By–product of oil manufacture, obtained from soya beans after extraction and appropriate heat treatment. (Urease activity maximum 0.4mg N/g x min.)	Protein Fibre, if > 8%
2.16	Soya (bean), dehulled, extracted, toasted	By–product of oil manufacture, obtained from dehulled soya beans after extraction and appropriate heat treatment. (Maximum fibre content 8% in the dry matter). (Urease activity maximum 0.5mg N/g x min.)	Protein
2.17	Soya (bean) protein concentrate	Product obtained from dehulled, fat extracted soya beans, subjected to a second extraction to reduce the level of nitrogen–free extract.	Protein
2.18	Vegetable oil[2]	Oil obtained from plants	Moisture, if > 1%.
2.19	Soya (bean) hulls	By–product obtained during dehulling of soya beans.	Fibre
2.20	Cotton seed	Seeds of cotton *Gossypium* spp. from which the fibres have been removed.	Protein Fibre Fat
2.21	Cotton seed, partially decorticated, extracted	By–product of oil manufacture, obtained by extraction of seeds of cotton from which the fibres and part of the husks have been removed. (Maximum fibre 22.5% in the dry matter).	Protein Fibre
2.22	Cotton seed expeller	By–product of oil manufacture, obtained by pressing of seeds of cotton from which the fibres have been removed.	Protein Fibre Fat
2.23	Niger seed expeller	By–product of oil manufacture, obtained by pressing of seeds of the niger plant *Guizotia abyssinica* (Lf) Cass. (Ash insoluble in HCl: maximum 3.4%)	Protein Fat Fibre
2.24	Sunflower seed	Seeds of the sunflower *Helianthus annuus* L.	
2.25	Sunflower seed, extracted	By–product of oil manufacture, obtained by extraction of seeds of the sunflower.	Protein
2.26	Sunflower seed, partially decorticated, extracted	By–product of oil manufacture, obtained by extraction of seeds of the sunflower from which part of the husks has been removed. (Maximum fibre 27.5% in the dry matter)	Protein Fibre

2.27	Linseed	Seeds of linseed *Linum usitatissimum* L. (Minimum botanical purity 93%)	
2.28	Linseed expeller	By–product of oil manufacture, obtained by pressing of linseed. (Minimum botanical purity 93%)	Protein Fat Fibre
2.29	Linseed, extracted	By–product of oil manufacture, obtained by extraction of linseed. (Minimum botanical purity 93%)	Protein
2.30	Olive pulp	By–product of oil manufacture, obtained by extraction of pressed olives *Olea europea* L. separated as far as possible from parts of the kernel	Protein Fibre
2.31	Sesame seed expeller	By–product of oil manufacture, obtained by pressing of seeds of the sesame plant *Sesamum indicum* L. (Ash insoluble in HCl: maximum 5%)	Protein Fibre Fat
2.32	Cocoa bean, partially decorticated, extracted	By–product of oil manufacture, obtained by extraction of dried and roasted cocoa beans *Theobroma cacao* L. from which part of the husks has been removed.	Protein Fibre
2.33	Cocoa husks	Teguments of the dried and roasted beans of *Theobroma cacao* L.	Fibre

[1] Where appropriate the indication 'low in glucosinolate' may be added. 'Low in glucosinolate' has the meaning given in Community legislation.

[2] The name must be supplemented by the plant species.

Number (1)	Name (2)	Description (3)	Compulsory declarations (4)
3. Legume seeds, their products and by–products			
3.01	Chick peas	Seeds of *Cicer arietinum* L.	
3.02	Guar meal, extracted	By–product obtained after extraction of the mucilage from seeds of *Cyanopsis tetragonoloba* (L.) Taub	Protein
3.03	Ervil	Seeds of *Ervum ervilia* L.	
3.04	Chickling vetch[1]	Seeds of *Lathyrus sativus* L. submitted to an appropriate heat treatment	
3.05	Lentils	Seeds of *Lens culinaris* a.o. Medik	
3.06	Sweet lupins	Seeds of *Lupinus* spp. Low in bitter seed content.	
3.07	Beans, toasted	Seeds of *Phaseolus* or *Vigna* spp. submitted to an appropriate heat treatment to destroy toxic lectines.	
3.08	Peas	Seeds of *Pisum* spp.	
3.09	Pea middlings	By–product obtained during the manufacture of pea-flour. It consists principally of particles of cotyledon, and to a lesser extent, of skins.	Protein Fibre
3.10	Pea bran	By–product obtained during the manufacture of pea meal. It is composed mainly of skins removed during the skinning and cleaning of peas.	Fibre
3.11	Horse beans	Seeds of *Vicia faba* L. spp. *faba* var. *equina Pers.* and var. *minuta (Alef.)* Mansf.	
3.12	Monantha vetch	Seeds of *Vicia monanthos* Desf.	
3.13	Vetches	Seeds of *Vicia sativa* L. var. *sativa* and other varieties	

[1] This name must be supplemented by an indication of the nature of the heat treatment.

Number (1)	Name (2)	Description (3)	Compulsory declarations (4)
4. Tubers, roots, their products and by–products			
4.01	(Sugar) beet pulp	By–product of the manufacture of sugar, consisting of extracted and dried pieces of sugar beet *Beta vulgaris* L. ssp. *vulgaris* var. *altissima* Doell. (Maximum content of ash insoluble in HCl: 4.5% of dry matter).	Content of ash insoluble in HCl, if > 3.5% of dry matter. Total sugar calculated as sucrose, if > 10.5%.
4.02	(Sugar) beet molasses	By–product consisting of the syrupy residue collected during the manufacture or refining of beet sugar.	Total sugar calculated as sucrose. Moisture, if > 28%.
4.03	(Sugar) beet pulp, molassed	By–product of the manufacture of sugar comprising dried sugar-beet pulp, to which molasses have been added. (Maximum content of ash insoluble in HCl: 4.5% of dry matter).	Total sugar calculated as sucrose. Content of ash insoluble in HCl, if > 3.5% of dry matter
4.04	(Sugar) beet vinasse	By–product obtained after the fermentation of beet molasses in the production of alcohol, yeast, citric acid and other organic substances	Protein Moisture, if > 35%
4.05	(Beet) sugar[1]	Sugar extracted from sugar beet	Sucrose
4.06	Sweet potato	Tubers of *Ipomoea batatas* (L.) Poir, regardless of their presentation	Starch
4.07	Manioc[2]	Roots of *Manibot esculenta* Crantz, regardless of their presentation. (Maximum content of ash insoluble in HCl: 4.5% of dry matter)	Starch Content of ash insoluble in HCl, if >3.5% of dry matter
4.08	Manioc starch[3], puffed	Starch obtained from manioc roots, greatly expanded by appropriate heat treatment.	Starch
4.09	Potato pulp	By–product of the manufacture of potato starch (*Solanum tuberosum* L.)	
4.10	Potato starch	Technically pure potato starch.	Starch
4.11	Potato protein	Dried by–product of starch manufacture composed mainly of protein substances obtained after the separation of starch.	Protein
4.12	Potato flakes	Product obtained by rotary drying of washed, peeled or unpeeled steamed potatoes.	Starch Fibre
4.13	Potato juice condensed	By–product of the manufacture of potato starch from which proteins and water have been partly removed.	Protein Ash
4.14	Pre–gelatinised potato starch	Product consisting of potato starch largely solubilised by heat treatment	Starch

[1] This name may be replaced by 'sucrose'.

[2] This name may be replaced by 'tapioca'.

[3] This name may be replaced by 'tapioca starch'.

23

Number (1)	Name (2)	Description (3)	Compulsory declarations (4)
5. Other seeds and fruits, their products and by-products			
5.01	Carob pods	Product obtained by crushing the dried fruits (pods) of the carob tree *Ceratonia seliqua* L., from which the locust beans have been removed.	Fibre
5.02	Citrus pulp	By-product obtained by pressing citrus fruit *Citrus* ssp. during the production of citrus juice.	Fibre
5.03	Fruit pulp[1]	By-product obtained by pressing pomaceous or stone fruit during the production of fruit juice.	Fibre
5.04	Tomato pulp	By-product obtained by pressing tomatoes *Solanum lycopersicum* Karst. during the production of tomato juice	Fibre
5.05	Grape pips, extracted	By-product obtained during the extraction of oil from grape pips	Fibre, if > 45%
5.06	Grape pulp	Grape pulp dried rapidly after the extraction of alcohol from which as much as possible of the stalks and pips have been removed	Fibre, if > 25%
5.07	Grape pips	Pips extracted from grape pulps, from which the oil has not been removed	Fat Fibre, if > 45%

[1] The name may be supplemented by the fruit species.

Number	Name	Description	Compulsory declarations
6. Forages and roughage			
6.01	Lucerne meal[1]	Product obtained by drying and milling young lucerne *Medicago sativa* L. and *Medicago* var. *Martyn*. It may contain up to 20% young clover or other forage crops dried and milled at the same time as the lucerne	Protein Fibre Ash insoluble in HC1, if > 3.5% of dry matter
6.02	Lucerne pomace	Dried by-product obtained by pressing of the juice from lucerne	Protein
6.03	Lucerne protein concentrate	Product obtained by artificially drying fractions of lucerne press juice, which has been centrifuged and heat treated to precipitate the proteins	Carotene Protein
6.04	Clover meal[1]	Product obtained by drying and milling young clover *Trifolium* spp. It may contain up to 20% young lucerne or other forage crops dried and milled at the same time as the clover	Protein Fibre Ash insoluble in HC1, if > 3.5% of dry matter
6.05	Grass meal[1][2]	Product obtained by drying and milling young forage plants	Protein Fibre Ash insoluble in HC1, if > 3.5% of dry matter
6.06	Cereals straw [3]	Straw of cereals	
6.07	Cereals straw, treated[4]	Product obtained by an appropriate treatment of cereals straw	Sodium, if treated with NaOH

[1] The term 'meal' may be replaced by 'pellets'. The method of drying may be added to the name.

[2] The species of forage crop may be added to the name.

[3] The cereal species must be indicated in the name.

[4] The name must be supplemented by an indication of the nature of the chemical treatment carried out.

Number (1)	Name (2)	Description (3)	Compulsory declarations (4)
7. Other plants, their products and by–products			
7.01	(Sugar) cane molasses	By–product consisting of the syrupy residue collected during the manufacture or refining of sugar from sugar cane *Saccharum officinarum* L.	Total sugar calculated as sucrose Moisture, if > 30%
7.02	(Sugar) cane vinasse	By–product obtained after the fermentation of cane molasses in the production of alcohol, yeast, citric acid or other organic substances.	Protein Moisture, if > 35%
7.03	(Cane) sugar[1]	Sugar extracted from sugar cane	Sucrose
7.04	Seaweed meal	Product obtained by drying and crushing seaweed, in particular brown seaweed. This product may have been washed to reduce the iodine content.	Ash

[1] This name may be replaced by 'sucrose'.

Number (1)	Name (2)	Description (3)	Compulsory declarations (4)
8. Milk products			
8.01	Skimmed-milk powder	Product obtained by drying milk from which most of the fat has been separated.	Protein Moisture, if > 5%
8.02	Buttermilk powder	Product obtained by drying the liquid which remains after butter churning.	Protein Fat Lactose Moisture, if > 6%
8.03	Whey powder	Product obtained by drying the liquid which remains after cheese, quark and casein making or similar processes.	Protein Lactose Moisture, if > 8% Ash
8.04	Whey powder, low in sugar	Product obtained by drying whey from which the lactose has been partly removed.	Protein Lactose Moisture, if > 8% Ash
8.05	Whey protein powder[1]	Product obtained by drying the protein compounds extracted from whey or milk by chemical or physical treatment	Protein Moisture, if > 8%
8.06	Casein powder	Product obtained from skimmed or buttermilk by drying casein precipitated by means of acids or rennet.	Protein Moisture, if > 10%
8.07	Lactose powder	The sugar separated from milk or whey by purification and drying.	Lactose Moisture, if > 5%.

[1] This name may be replaced by 'milk albumin powder'.

Number (1)	Name (2)	Description (3)	Compulsory declarations (4)
9. Land animal products			
9.01	Meat meal[1]	Product obtained by heating, drying and grinding whole or parts of warm-blooded land animals from which the fat may have been partially extracted or physically removed. The product must be substantially free of hooves, horn, bristle, hair and feathers, as well as digestive tract content (minimum protein content 50% in dry matter). (Maximum total phosphorus content: 8%)	Protein Fat Ash Moisture, if > 8%
9.02	Meat-and-bone meal[1]	Product obtained by heating, drying and grinding whole or parts of warm-blooded land animals from which the fat may have been partially extracted or physically removed. The product must be substantially free of hooves, horn, bristle, hair and feathers, as well as digestive tract content	Protein Fat Ash Moisture, if > 8%
9.03	Bone meal	Product obtained by heating, drying and finely grinding bones of warm-blooded land animals from which the fat has been largely extracted or physically removed. The product must be substantially free of hooves, horn, bristle, hair and feathers, as well as digestive tract content	Protein Ash Moisture, if > 8%
9.04	Greaves	Residual product of the manufacture of tallow, lard and other extracted or physically removed fats of animal origin	Protein Fat Moisture, if > 8%
9.05	Poultry meal[1]	Product obtained by heating, drying and grinding by-products from slaughtered poultry. The product must be substantially free of feathers	Protein Fat Ash Ash insoluble in HCl if > 3.3% Moisture, if > 8%
9.06	Feather meal, hydrolysed	Product obtained by hydrolysing, drying and grinding poultry feathers	Protein Ash insoluble in HCl if > 3.4% Moisture, if > 8%
9.07	Blood meal	Product obtained by drying the blood of slaughtered warm-blooded animals. The product must be substantially free of foreign matter	Protein Moisture, if > 8%
9.08	Animal fat[2]	Product composed of fat from warm-blooded land animals	Moisture, if > 1%

[1] Products containing more than 13% fat in the dry matter must be qualified as 'rich in fat'.

[2] This name may be supplemented by a more accurate description of the type of animal fat depending on its origin or production process (tallow, lard, bone fat, etc.).

Number (1)	Name (2)	Description (3)	Compulsory declarations (4)
10. Fish, other marine animals, their products and by-products			
10.01	Fish meal[1]	Product obtained by processing whole or parts of fish from which part of the oil may have been removed and to which fish solubles may have been re-added.	Protein Fat Ash, if > 20% Moisture, if > 8%
10.02	Fish solubles, condensed	Product obtained during manufacture of fish meal which has been separated and stabilised by acidification or drying.	Protein Fat Moisture, if > 5%
10.03	Fish oil	Oil obtained from fish or parts of fish.	Moisture if > 1%
10.04	Fish oil, refined, hardened	Oil obtained from fish or parts of fish which has been refined and subjected to hydrogenation.	Iodine number Moisture, if > 1%

[1] Products containing more than 75% protein in the dry matter may be qualified as 'rich in protein'.

Number	Name	Description	Compulsory declarations
11. Minerals			
11.01	Calcium carbonate[1]	Product obtained by grinding sources of calcium carbonate, such as limestone, oyster or mussel shells, or by precipitation from acid solution.	Calcium Ash insoluble in HCl if > 5%
11.02	Calcium and magnesium carbonate	Natural mixture of calcium carbonate and magnesium carbonate	Calcium Magnesium
11.03	Calcareous marine algae (Maerl)	Product of natural origin obtained from calcareous algae, ground or granulated.	Calcium Ash insoluble in HCl if > 5%
11.04	Magnesium oxide	Technically pure magnesium oxide (MgO)	Magnesium
11.05	Magnesium sulphate	Technically pure magnesium sulphate ($MgSO_4.7H_2O$)	Magnesium Sulphur
11.06	Dicalcium phosphate[2]	Precipitated calcium monohydrogen phosphate from bones or inorganic sources ($CaHPO_4.xH_2O$)	Calcium Total phosphorus
11.07	Mono-dicalcium phosphate	Product obtained chemically and composed of equal parts of dicalcium phosphate and mono-calcium phosphate ($CaHPO_4-Ca(H_2PO_4)_2.H_2O$	Total phosphorus Calcium
11.08	Defluorinated rock phosphate	Product obtained by grinding purified and appropriately defluorinated natural phosphates.	Total phosphorus Calcium
11.09	Degelatinised bone meal	Degelatinsed, sterilised and ground bones from which the fat has been removed	Total phosphorus Calcium
11.11	Calcium-magnesium phosphate	Technically pure calcium-magnesium phosphate	Calcium Magnesium Total phosphorus
11.12	Mono-ammonium phosphate	Technically pure mono-ammonium phosphate ($NH_4H_2PO_4$)	Total nitrogen Total phosphorus

11.13	Sodium chloride[1]	Technically pure sodium chloride or product obtained by grinding natural sources of sodium chloride, such as (rock) and (marine) salt	Sodium
11.14	Magnesium propionate	Technically pure magnesium propionate	Magnesium
11.15	Magnesium phosphate	Product consisting of technically pure (dibasic) magnesium phosphate ($MgHPO_4.xH_2O$)	Total phosphorus Magnesium
11.16	Sodium-calcium-magnesium phosphate	Product consisting of sodium-calcium-magnesium phosphate	Total phosphorus Magnesium Calcium Sodium
11.17	Mono-sodium phosphate	Technically pure mono–sodium phosphate ($NaH_2PO.H_2O$)	Total phosphorus Sodium
11.18	Sodium bicarbonate	Technically pure sodium bicarbonate ($NaHCO_3$)	Sodium

[1] The nature of the source may be indicated additionally in the name or replace it.

[2] The manufacturing process may be included in the name.

Number (1)	Name (2)	Description (3)	Compulsory declarations (4)
12. Miscellaneous			
12.01	Bakery and pasta products and by–products[1]	Product or by–product obtained from the manufacture of bread, including fine bakers' wares, biscuits or pasta	Starch Total sugar calculated as sucrose
12.02	Confectionery products and by–products[1]	Product or by–product obtained from the manufacture of confectionery including chocolate	Total sugar calculated as sucrose
12.03	Products and by–products of pastry and ice-cream making[1]	Product or by–product obtained from the manufacture of pastry, cakes or ice-cream.	Starch Total sugar expressed as sucrose Fat
12.04	Fatty acids	By–product obtained during the deacidification, by means of lye or by distillation of oils and fats of unspecified vegetable or animal origin.	Fat Moisture, if > 1%
12.05	Salts of fatty acids[2]	Product obtained by saponification of fatty acids with calcium, sodium or potassium hydroxide.	Fat Ca (or Na or K, when appropriate)

[1] The name may be amended or supplemented to specify the agri–food process from which the feed material was obtained.

[2] The name may be supplemented by an indication of the salt obtained.

PART III

OTHER FEED MATERIAL

	Feed material (1)	Compulsory declaration (2)
1.	Cereal grains	
2.	Products and by–products of cereal grains	Starch, if > 20% Protein, if > 10% Fat, if >5% Fibre
3.	Oil seeds, oil fruits	
4.	Products and by–products of oil seeds, oil fruits	Protein, if > 10% Fat, if >5% Fibre
5.	Legume seeds	
6.	Products and by–products of legume seeds	Protein, if > 10% Fibre
7.	Tubers, roots	
8.	Products and by–products of tubers and roots	Starch Fibre Ash insoluble in HC1, if > 3.5%
9.	Other products and by–products of the sugar beet processing industry	Fibre, if > 15% Total sugar, calculated as sucrose Ash insoluble in HC1, if > 3.5%
10.	Other seeds and fruits, their products and by–products	Protein Fibre Fat, if > 10%
11.	Forages and roughage	Protein, if > 10% Fibre
12.	Other plants, their products and by–products	Protein, if > 10% Fibre
13.	Products and by–products of the sugar cane processing industry	Fibre, if > 15% Total sugar calculated as sucrose
14.	Milk products and by–products	Protein Moisture, if > 5% Lactose, if > 10%
15.	Land animal products	Protein, if > 10% Fat, if > 5% Moisture, if > 8%
16.	Fish, other marine animals, their products and by–products	Protein, if > 10% Fat, if > 5% Moisture, if > 8%
17.	Minerals	Relevant minerals
18.	Miscellaneous	Protein, if > 10% Fibre Fat, if > 10% Starch, if > 30% Total sugar, calculated as sucrose, if > 10%

CONTENTS OF THE STATUTORY STATEMENT OR OTHER DECLARATION (EXCEPT FOR ADDITIVES AND PREMIXTURES NOT CONTAINED IN FEEDING STUFFS)

PART I

Interpretation

1. The expression "in the case of any compound feeding stuff", wherever it appears in this Schedule, shall be construed as referring to any compound feeding stuff which is put into circulation.

Additive declarations (applicable to all feeding stuffs)

2. Where any person puts into circulation any feeding stuff to which there has been added in the course of manufacture or preparation for putting into circulation, an additive of any of the kinds specified below (other than as an authorised medicated pre-mix or an authorised intermediate product within the meaning of Council Directive 90/167/EEC(**a**)) and which is not excluded from application of the Additives Directive by Article 22 of that Directive (concerning exports to third countries), the following particulars shall be contained in the statutory statement—

(a) for antioxidants, colourants or preservatives—

    (i) if the feeding stuff is a compound feeding stuff other than a pet food, the name of the additive;

    (ii) if the feeding stuff is a pet food and it is not covered by paragraph (iii) below, the words "with antioxidant", "coloured with" or "colourant", or "preservative" or "preserved with", as appropriate, followed by the name of the additive; and

    (iii) if the feeding stuff is a pet food, it is put up in a package having a net weight not exceeding 10 kilograms, its statutory statement contains a reference number by means of which the feeding stuff concerned may be identified, and its manufacturer supplies, on request, details of the name of the additive concerned,—

        (aa) the particulars specified in paragraph (ii) above, or

        (bb) the words "with antioxidant", "coloured with" or "preserved with", as appropriate, followed by the word "EC additives";

(b) for vitamin A, D or E, the name of the vitamin, and the active substance level (in the case of vitamin A or D) or the alpha-tocopherol level as acetate (in the case of vitamin E), whether naturally present or added, together in either case with an indication of the period during which that level will remain present but where more than one of these vitamins is present, either the period for each or only the shortest of such periods;

(c) for copper, the name of the additive and the total level of the element, whether naturally present or added;

(d) for enzymes—

    (i) the names of the active constituents according to their enzymatic activities, as specified in the authorisation concerned;

    (ii) the identification number allotted by the International Union of Biochemistry;

    (iii) the activity units (expressed as activity units per kilogram or activity units per litre);

    (iv) an indication of the period during which the activity units will remain present;

    (v) an indication of any significant characteristics of the enzyme arising during manufacture, as specified in the authorisation concerned; and

    (vi) the EC registration number;

(e) for micro-organisms—

    (i) the identification of each strain, in accordance with the authorisation;

    (ii) the file number of each strain;

    (iii) the number of colony-forming units (expressed as CFU/kg);

    (iv) the EC registration number;

    (v) an indication of the period during which the colony-forming units will remain present; and

    (vi) an indication of any significant characteristics of the micro-organisms arising during manufacture, as specified in the authorisation concerned.

3. In relation to the additives specified below the following particulars may be contained in the statutory statement in addition to those required by paragraph 2—

(a) for trace elements other than copper (if the amount present can be determined by the method of

---

(**a**) Council Directive 90/167/EEC (OJ No. L92, 7.4.1990, p. 42) laying down the conditions governing the preparation, placing on the market and use of medicated feedingstuffs in the Community.

analysis specified in Point 3 of the Annex to Directive 78/633/EEC(a) or by some other valid scientific method), the name of the additive and the total level of the element, whether naturally present or added; and

(b) for vitamins other than vitamins A, D and E, provitamins and substances having a similar chemical effect (if the amount present can be determined by any valid scientific method), the name of the additive, the active substance level, whether naturally present or added, and an indication of the period during which that level will remain present.

4. Any amount referred to—

(a) in paragraph 2(c), (3)(a) or 3(b) shall be expressed in milligrams per kilogram; and

(b) in paragraph 2(b) shall be expressed in million international units per kilogram, international units per kilogram, milligrams per kilogram or micrograms per kilogram, as appropriate.

5. By way of exception to paragraph 4(a), any amount referred to in paragraph 2(c), 3(a) or 3(b) may be expressed as a percentage by weight, unless the amount is less than 0.1% by weight, in which case it shall be expressed in milligrams per kilogram or micrograms per kilogram as appropriate.

6. The particulars required or permitted by paragraphs 2 or 3 to be included in the statutory statement may be accompanied (in the case of any additive not being an enzyme or a micro-organism) by the trade name or the EC registration number of any additive named therein.

Warning statements

7. Where any person puts into circulation any feed material comprising protein derived from mammalian tissue but containing no mammalian meat and bone meal, and intended for animals other than pet animals, the statutory statement shall contain the following declaration—

"This feed material comprises protein derived from mammalian tissue the feeding of which to ruminants is prohibited".

8. Where any person puts into circulation any feed material comprising or containing mammalian meat and bone meal, and intended for animals other than pet animals, the statutory statement shall contain the following declaration—

"This feed material comprises protein derived from mammalian tissue the feeding of which to ruminants, all other categories of farmed creatures and equine animals is prohibited".

9. In the case of any compound feeding stuff containing protein derived from mammalian tissue but containing no mammalian meat and bone meal, and intended for animals other than pet animals, the statutory statement shall contain the following declaration—

"This compound feeding stuff contains protein derived from mammalian tissue the feeding of which to ruminants is prohibited".

10. In the case of any compound feeding stuff containing mammalian meat and bone meal, and intended for animals other than pet animals, the statutory statement shall contain the following declaration—

"This compound feeding stuff contains protein derived from mammalian tissue the feeding of which to ruminants, all other categories of farmed creatures and equine animals is prohibited."

Feed materials

11. Subject to paragraphs 12 to 15, in the case of any feed material which is put into circulation by any person the following particulars shall be contained in the statutory statement—

(a) in the case of any feed material of a kind specified in column (3) of Part II to Schedule 2—

(i) the corresponding name specified in column (2) of that Part (the inclusion of any word appearing in brackets in that column being optional); and

(ii) the particulars (if any) specified in relation to the feed material in the corresponding entry in column (4) of that Part;

(b) in the case of any feed material of a kind specified in column (1) of Part III to Schedule 2—

(i) its name or description there specified, or a name and description (other than one specified in that column, or in column (2) of Part II to that Schedule) sufficiently specific to indicate the nature of the material, and in conformity with the criteria specified in the Introductory Notes to Part II to that Schedule; and

(ii) the particulars specified in relation to the feed material in the corresponding entry in column (2) of Part III to that Schedule;

(c) in the case of any feed material—

(i) subject to regulation 9(5) as read with Article 6(4) of the Feed Materials Directive, which shall be observed where applicable, the words "feed material";

(a)   OJ No. L206, 29.7.78, p. 43.

31

(ii) the moisture content of the feed material, if it exceeds 14% by weight of the feed material or, where a different percentage is specified in relation to that feed material in Part II or Part III to Schedule 2, if it exceeds that percentage;

(iii) the moisture content of the feed material, where it does not exceed the relevant percentage specified in paragraph (ii), but a purchaser requests that the moisture content be declared;

(iv) the level of ash soluble in hydrochloric acid in the feed material, if that level exceeds 2.2% in the dry matter or, where a different percentage is specified in relation to that feed material in Part II or Part III to Schedule 2, if it exceeds that percentage;

(v) where any other feed material has been used to denature the feed material, the nature and quantity of the other feed material so used;

(vi) where any other feed material has been used to bind the feed material, the nature of the other feed material so used;

(vii) the net quantity of the feed material, expressed in units of mass in the case of any solid feed material and, in the case of any liquid feed material, in units of mass or volume;

(viii) where the feed material is part of a divided batch of feed materials, reference to the original batch;

(ix) the name or business name, and the address or registered business address, of the person within the European Community responsible for the particulars specified in this sub-paragraph, if the establishment referred to in sub-paragraph (x) is not responsible for them; and

(x) where the establishment producing the feed material must be approved in accordance with Regulation (EC) No 1774/2002 of the European Parliament and of the Council laying down health rules concerning animal by-products not intended for human consumption(**a**); the name or business name, and the address or registered business address, of the establishment, the approval number, the batch reference number or any other particulars which ensure that the material can be traced.

12. The particulars specified in paragraph 11(a)(ii) and (b)(ii) and (c)(ii) to (iv) shall not be required where—

(a) before the feed material concerned is supplied, the person to whom it is supplied notifies the supplier in writing that those particulars need not be supplied, or

(b) any feed material of animal or vegetable origin, fresh or preserved, and intended for pet animals, is supplied (in a quantity not exceeding 10 kg) directly to the final user thereof, by a person established in the United Kingdom.

13.—(1) In the case of any feed material which—

(a) originated in a third country, and

(b) is, for the first time, put into circulation in England and the European Community,

in the circumstances specified in the introductory paragraph of Article 6(2) of the Feed Materials Directive, provisional details of the particulars specified in paragraph 11(a)(ii), (b)(ii) and (c)(ii) to (iv) may be provided, if the requirements of sub-paragraph (2) below are observed.

(2) The requirements of this sub-paragraph are observed if—

(a) the person responsible for giving those particulars gives notification, in advance, of the impending arrival of the feed material in England, to an inspector appointed under section 67(3) by the authority which, by virtue of section 67(1), has the duty to enforce Part IV of the Act at the intended place of arrival;

(b) the provisional details are accompanied by the following declaration in bold type—
"provisional data to be confirmed by .... (name and address of the laboratory instructed to carry out the analyses) regarding .... (reference number of the sample to be analysed) before .... date;" and

(c) the person responsible as mentioned in subparagraph (a) provides the final particulars in question to the person to whom the feed material is supplied, and to the inspector referred to in sub-paragraph (a), within 10 days of its arrival in England.

(3) Where the requirements of sub-paragraph (2) are observed, it shall be the duty of the inspector concerned to notify the European Commission that, in relation to the feed material concerned, the provisional particulars concerned have been provided, and to inform the Commission of the nature of those particulars.

(**a**) OJ No. L273, 10.10.2002, p. 1.

14.—(1) The particulars specified in paragraph 11 shall not be required in the case of any feed material of animal or vegetable origin, in its natural state, fresh or preserved, and which is not treated with an additive other than any preservative, if the feed material is provided by a farmer-producer to a breeder-user, both of whom carry on business in the United Kingdom.

(2) For the purposes of this paragraph, "farmer-producer" and "breeder-user" shall have the same meaning as in the Feed Materials Directive.

15.—(1) The particulars specified in paragraph 11(a)(ii), (b)(ii), and (c)(ii) to (vii) shall not be required in the case of any feed material which is a by-product of vegetable or animal origin derived from agro-industrial processing, and which has a moisture content greater than 50%.

(2) For the purposes of this paragraph, "agro-industrial processing" shall have the same meaning as in the Feed Materials Directive.

16.—(1) Subject to sub-paragraph (2), in the case of any feed material which is put into circulation by any person, information may be provided in addition to the particulars required or permitted to be contained in the statutory statement or otherwise declared.

(2) Any such information provided in addition to the particulars required or permitted to be contained in the statutory statement or otherwise declared—

(a) shall be clearly separated from those particulars;

(b) shall relate to objective or quantifiable factors which can be substantiated; and

(c) shall not be misleading.

Compound feeding stuffs: general

17.—(1) Subject to sub-paragraph (2), in the case of any compound feeding stuff, the following particulars shall be contained in the statutory statement—

(a) the description "complete feeding stuff", "complementary feeding stuff", "mineral feeding stuff", "molassed feeding stuff", "complete milk replacer feed" or "complementary milk replacer feed" as appropriate;

(b) the species or category of animal for which the feeding stuff is intended and directions for the proper use of the feeding stuff, indicating the purpose for which it is intended, except where the feeding stuff is constituted from no more than three ingredients and is clearly described by reference to its ingredients, either in the statutory statement or elsewhere on its package, label or container; and

(c) the name or trade name and address or registered office of the person established in the European Community responsible for the accuracy of the particulars which, in accordance with this Schedule are required in the case of compound feeding stuffs to be contained in the statutory statement or otherwise declared.

(2) In the case of—

(a) any pet food, the descriptions "complete pet food" and "complementary pet food" may be used instead of "complete feeding stuff" and "complementary feeding stuff" respectively;

(b) any feeding stuff for pet animals other than dogs or cats, each of the descriptions "complete feeding stuff" and "complementary feeding stuff" may be replaced by either of the descriptions "compound feeding stuff" or "compound pet food", but in such a case the statutory statement shall comply with paragraph 19 below and the provisions relating to complete feeding stuffs in Part II of this Schedule, even if it would not otherwise be required to do so.

18. In the case of any compound feeding stuff, the following particulars shall be declared either in the statutory statement, or elsewhere on the package, label or container (in which case the statutory statement shall indicate where they are to be found)—

(a) the net quantity, expressed in the case of solid products in units of mass, and in the case of liquid products in units of mass or volume;

(b) the minimum storage life, which shall be expressed—

(i) in the case of microbiologically highly perishable feeding stuffs, by the words "use before . . ." followed by the appropriate date (day, month and year), and

(ii) in all other cases by the words "best before . . ." followed by the appropriate date (month and year),

except that, where an expiry date for a period is required to be declared by paragraph 2(b) or 3(b), and is earlier than the appropriate date otherwise required by this paragraph, that expiry date shall be used as the appropriate date;

(c) the batch reference number; and

(d) the approval or registration number allocated by the relevant enforcement authority to the establishment which manufactured the compound feeding stuff.

19.—(1) In the case of any compound feeding stuff other than a whole grain mix, the statutory statement—

    (a) shall include such declarations of the matters provided for in the columns of Part II of this Schedule as must be included; and

    (b) may include such declarations provided for in the columns of Part II of this Schedule as may be included,

for consistency with Article 5 of the Compound Feedingstuffs Directive.

(2) In the case of a whole grain mix which is put into circulation, the statutory statement may include such of the declarations provided for in the columns of Part II of this Schedule as may be included for consistency with Article 5 of the Compound Feedingstuffs Directive.

20.—(1) In the case of any compound feeding stuff other than a whole grain mix, the moisture content shall be declared in the statutory statement if it exceeds the following levels—

milk replacer feeds and other compound feeding stuffs with a milk product content exceeding 40%	7%
mineral feeding stuffs containing no organic substances	5%
mineral feeding stuffs containing organic substances	10%
other compound feeding stuffs	14%

(2) In the case of a whole grain mix, or a compound feeding stuff with a moisture content not exceeding the limits stated in sub-paragraph (1) which is put into circulation, the moisture content may be declared in the statutory statement.

21. In the case of any compound feeding stuff having a level of ash insoluble in hydrochloric acid not exceeding the relevant level specified in regulation 18(1)(a) or, as the case may be, (b), that level may be declared in the statutory statement as a percentage of the feeding stuff as such.

22. In the case of any compound feeding stuff, the following particulars may be included in the statutory statement—

    (a) if the manufacturer is not the person responsible for the labelling particulars, the name or business name and the address or registered business address of the manufacturer;

    (b) an indication of the physical condition of the feeding stuff or the specific processing it has undergone;

    (c) the date of manufacture, expressed as follows—

        "manufactured . . . [days, months or years] before the minimum storage life expiry date indicated . . . [place where indicated if not on statutory statement].";

    (d) the identification mark or trade mark of the person responsible for the particulars which, in accordance with this Schedule, are required or permitted in the case of compound feeding stuffs to be contained in the statutory statement or otherwise declared;

    (e) the description or trade name of the feeding stuff;

    (f) the price of the feeding stuff; and

    (g) the country of origin or manufacture of the feeding stuff.

23.—(1) In the particulars required or permitted by paragraphs 18 to 21 and 25 and by paragraph 19 of Schedule 4 to the 2000 Regulations to be set out in the statutory statement—

    (a) unless the paragraph in question specifies some other method of expression, the amounts shown shall be expressed in each case as a percentage of the weight of the feeding stuff as such; and

    (b) phosphorus shall be expressed as "phosphorus P".

(2) An expression of an amount as being within a range of percentages set out in the statutory statement shall not be regarded as compliance with sub-paragraph (1).

24.—(1) Subject to sub-paragraph (2), in the case of any compound feeding stuff, information may be provided in addition to the particulars required or permitted to be contained in the statutory statement or otherwise declared.

(2) Any information provided pursuant to sub-paragraph (1)—

    (a) shall be clearly separated from those particulars;

    (b) shall not be designed to indicate the presence or content of analytical constituents other than those the declaration of which is provided for in this Schedule or in Schedule 7;

    (c) shall relate to objective or quantifiable factors which can be substantiated;

    (d) shall not be misleading, in particular by attributing to the feeding stuff effects or properties that it does not possess, or by suggesting that it possesses special characteristics, when all similar feeding stuffs contain similar properties;

    (e) shall not claim that the feeding stuff will prevent, treat or cure a disease;

    (f) shall not, in the case of any feeding stuff intended for a particular nutritional purpose, include a generic description other than in the form of the generic term "dietetic";

(g) shall not, in the case of any feeding stuff other than one intended for a particular nutritional purpose, include a generic description in that form; and

(h) shall not include reference to a particular pathological condition, unless—

   (i) the feeding stuff is intended for a particular nutritional purpose, and

   (ii) the particular nutritional purpose is specified in respect of that feeding stuff in column 1 of Chapter A of Schedule 7 and relates to that condition.

Compound pet food: specific provisions

25.—(1) In the case of any compound feeding stuff for dogs or cats, all the feed materials shall be declared in the statutory statement.

(2) In the case of any compound feeding stuff for pet animals other than dogs and cats, the feed materials may be declared in the statutory statement, and in such case all the feed materials shall be declared.

(3) Subject to paragraph 29(2) below and paragraph 3 of Chapter B of Schedule 7, feed materials declared in accordance with sub-paragraph (1) or (2) above shall be declared either—

(a) by their specific names, with an indication of the amount of each feed material; or

(b) by their specific names in descending order by weight; or

(c) by categories, as described in Part I of Schedule 8, in descending order by weight,

and the use of one of those forms of declaration shall preclude the use of either of the others, except—

   (i) where the declaration is by categories and any feed material belongs to none of the categories described in Part I of Schedule 8, in which case that feed material, designated by its specific name, shall be listed in order by weight in relation to the categories; or

   (ii) in the case of any feeding stuff intended for a particular nutritional purpose, paragraph 29(2) below and paragraph 3 of Chapter B of Schedule 7 require the declaration of any feed material by its specific name, in which case any feed material to which those provisions do not apply may be declared by reference to the category to which it belongs.

26. Where any declaration under paragraph 25 or under paragraph 19 of Schedule 4 to the 2000 Regulations is by specific names, any feed material described in column 3 of Part II of Schedule 2 shall be declared by the corresponding name specified in column 2 of that Part (the inclusion of any word appearing in brackets in that column being optional).

Complementary feeding stuffs

27.—(1) In the case of any complementary feeding stuff which, subject to Article 10 of the Additives Regulation, is put into circulation and contains any additive in excess of the maximum content in relation to complete feeding stuffs specified for that additive in the relevant Part of Parts I to VIII of the Table to Schedule 3 to the 2000 Regulations or, as the case may be, in the relevant European Community Regulation, and which is not covered by Article 22 (concerning exports to third countries) of the Additives Directive, the instructions for use in the statutory statement shall state, according to the species and age of the animal, the maximum quantity in grams or kilograms of the feeding stuff which, under these Regulations, may be given per animal per day, and shall be so formulated that, when they are correctly followed, the final content of the additive in relation to complete feeding stuffs does not exceed the maximum so specified in relation to them.

(2) Sub-paragraph (1) shall not apply to any products delivered to manufacturers of compound feeding stuffs or to their suppliers.

Ingredients to which particular attention is drawn

28.—(1) Subject to sub-paragraph (2), in the case of any compound pet food, or of any feeding stuff intended for a particular nutritional purpose for animals other than pet animals which is put into circulation, particular attention may be drawn in the statutory statement, or elsewhere on the package, label or container, to the presence or low content of one or more ingredients which are essential aspects of the characteristics of the feeding stuff.

(2) Where particular attention is drawn to the presence or low content of any ingredient, as permitted by sub-paragraph (1), the minimum or maximum content, expressed in terms of the percentage by weight of that ingredient, shall be clearly indicated—

(a) opposite the statement which draws attention to that presence or low content;

(b) in the list of ingredients; or

(c) by mentioning that presence or low content and the percentage thereof (by weight) opposite the corresponding category of ingredients.

35

Feeding stuffs for particular nutritional purposes

29.—(1) Subject to sub-paragraph (2), in the case of any feeding stuff intended for a particular nutritional purpose which is put into circulation, the following particulars shall be contained in the statutory statement—

(a) the term "dietetic";

(b) a description of the feeding stuff;

(c) the particular nutritional purpose of the feeding stuff, as specified in column 1 of Chapter A of Schedule 7;

(d) the essential nutritional characteristics of the feeding stuff, as specified in column 2 of that Chapter;

(e) the declarations prescribed in column 4 of that Chapter;

(f) the declarations, if any, prescribed in column 6 of that Chapter;

(g) where any declarations prescribed in that column do not include a declaration that it is recommended that the prior opinion of a veterinarian be sought, the words "It is recommended that a specialist's opinion be sought before use"; and

(h) the recommended length of time for use of the feeding stuff.

(2) The particulars required by sub-paragraph (1) to be contained in the statutory statement shall be declared in accordance with the requirements of paragraphs 3–7 and 9 of Chapter B of Schedule 7.

30.—(1) Subject to sub-paragraph (2), in the case of any feeding stuff intended for a particular nutritional purpose which is put into circulation, particular attention may be drawn in the statutory statement, or elsewhere on the package, label or container, to the presence or low content of one or more analytical constituents which are essential aspects of the characteristics of the feeding stuff.

(2) Where particular attention is drawn to the presence or low content of any analytical constituent, as permitted by sub-paragraph (1), the maximum or minimum content, expressed in terms of the percentage by weight of that analytical constituent, shall be clearly indicated in the list of analytical constituents.

Permitted protein products

31.—(1) In the case of any product named as a permitted product in column 2 of Schedule 6, the statutory statement shall contain, in addition to any other particulars required by these Regulations, the name specified for that product in column 7 of that Schedule, together with such further particulars as may be specified in that column in relation to it.

(2) In the case of any compound feeding stuff containing, for use as a protein source, any product named as a permitted product in column 2 of Schedule 6, the statutory statement shall contain, in addition to any other particulars required by these Regulations, the name specified for that product in column 7 of that Schedule, together with such further particulars as may be specified in that column in relation to compound feeding stuffs containing that product.

PART II

DECLARATION OF ANALYTICAL CONSTITUENTS

Feeding stuffs	Analytical constituents and levels	Species or category of animal	
Column 1	Column 2	Column 3 Compulsory Declarations	Column 4 Optional Declarations
Complete feeding stuffs	– Protein	} Animals except pets other than dogs and cats	} Pets other than dogs and cats
	– Oils and fats	}	}
	– Fibre	}	}
	– Ash	}	}
	– Lysine	Pigs	Animals other than pigs
	– Methionine	Poultry	Animals other than poultry
	– Cystine	....	}
	– Threonine	....	}
	– Tryptophan	....	}
	– Energy value	....	Poultry (calculated according to EEC method – see Schedule 1)
		....	Pigs and ruminants (calculated according to national official methods – see Schedule 1)
	– Starch	....	}
	– Total sugar (as sucrose)	....	}
	Total sugar plus starch	....	}
	– Calcium	....	} All animals
	– Sodium	....	}
	– Magnesium	....	}
	– Potassium	....	}
	– Phosphorus	Fish except ornamental fish	Animals other than fish except ornamental fish
Complementary feeding stuffs – Mineral	– Protein	....	}
	– Fibre	....	}
	– Ash	....	}
	– Oils and fats	....	} All animals
	– Lysine	....	}
	– Methionine	....	}
	– Cystine	....	}
	– Threonine	....	}
	– Tryptophan	....	}
	– Calcium	}	
	– Phosphorus	} All animals	

Feeding stuffs	Analytical constituents and levels	Species or category of animal	
Column 1	Column 2	Column 3 Compulsory Declarations	Column 4 Optional Declarations
	– Sodium	} Ruminants	
	– Magnesium		Animals other than ruminants
	– Potassium	....	All animals
Complementary feeding stuffs – Molassed	– Protein	}	
	– Fibre	}	
	– Total sugar (as sucrose)	} All animals	
	– Ash	}	
	– Oils and fats	....	All animals
	– Calcium	....	}
	– Phosphorous	....	} All animals
	– Sodium	....	}
	– Potassium	....	}
	– Magnesium ≥ 0.5%	Ruminants	Animals other than ruminants
	< 0.5%	....	All animals
Complementary feeding stuffs – Other	– Protein	}	}
	– Oils and fats	} Animals except pets other than dogs and cats	} Pets other than dogs and cats
	– Fibre	}	}
	– Ash	}	}
	– Calcium ≥ 5%	Animals other than pets	Pets
	< 5%	....	All animals
	– Phosphorus ≥ 2%	Animals other than pets	Pets
	< 2%	....	All animals
	– Magnesium ≥ 0.5%	Ruminants	Animals other than ruminants
	< 0.5%	....	}
	– Sodium	....	} All animals
	– Potassium	....	}
	– Energy value	....	Poultry (declaration according to EEC method – see Schedule 1)
		....	Pigs and ruminants (declaration according to national official methods – see Schedule 1)
	– Lysine	Pigs	Animals other than pigs
	– Methionine	Poultry	Animals other than poultry

Feeding stuffs	Analytical constituents and levels	Species or category of animal	
Column 1	Column 2	Column 3 Compulsory Declarations	Column 4 Optional Declarations
	– Cystine	.... }	
	– Threonine	.... }	
	– Tryptophan	.... }	
	– Starch	.... }	
	– Total sugar (as sucrose)	.... }	All animals
	– Total sugar plus starch	.... }	

39

LIMITS OF VARIATION

PART A

COMPOUND FEEDING STUFFS EXCEPT THOSE FOR PETS

Analytical constituents	Limits of variation (absolute value in percentage by weight, except where otherwise specified)
Ash	If present in excess — 2 for declarations of 10% or more 20% of the amount stated for declarations of 5% or more but less than 10% 1 for declarations of less than 5% In the case of deficiency — 3 for declarations of 10% or more 30% of the amount stated for declarations of 5% or more but less than 10% 1.5 for declarations less than 5%
Ash insoluble in hydrochloric acid	If present in excess — 2 for declarations of 10% or more 20% of the amount stated for declarations of 4% or more but less than 10% 1 for declarations of less than 4%
Calcium	If present in excess — 3.6 for declarations of 16% or more 22.5% of the amount stated for declarations of 12% or more but less than 16% 2.7 for declarations of 6% or more but less than 12% 45% of the amount stated for declarations of 1% or more but less than 6% 0.45 for declarations less than 1% In case of deficiency — 1.2% for declarations of 16% or more 7.5% of the amount stated for declarations of 12% or more but less than 16% 0.9 for declarations of 6% or more but less than 12% 15% of the amount stated for declarations of 1% or more but less than 6% 0.15 for declarations less than 1%
Cystine	In case of deficiency — 30% of the amount stated
Fibre	If present in excess —

Analytical constituents	Limits of variation (absolute value in percentage by weight, except where otherwise specified)
	1.8 for declarations of 12% or more
	15% of the amount stated for declarations of 6% or more but less than 12%
	0.9 for declarations of less than 6%
	In case of deficiency —
	5.4 for declarations of 12% or more
	45% of the amount stated for declarations of 6% or more but less than 12%
	2.7 for declarations of less than 6%
Lysine	In case of deficiency —
	30% of the amount stated
Magnesium	If present in excess —
	4.5 for declarations of 15% or more
	30% of the amount stated for declarations of 7.5% or more but less than 15%
	2.25 for declarations of 5% or more but less than 7.5%
	45% of the amount stated for declarations of 0.7% or more but less than 5%
	0.3 for declarations less than 0.7%
	In case of deficiency —
	1.5 for declarations of 15% or more
	10% of the amount stated for declarations of 7.5% or more but less than 15%
	0.75 for declarations of 5% or more but less than 7.5%
	15% of the amount stated for declarations of 0.7% or more but less than 5%
	0.1 for declarations less than 0.7%
Methionine	In case of deficiency —
	30% of the amount stated
Moisture	If present in excess —
	1 for declarations of 10% or more
	10% of the amount stated for declarations of 5% or more but less than 10%
	0.5 for declarations less than 5%
Oils and fats	If present in excess —
	3 for declarations of 15% or more
	20% of the amount stated for declarations of 8% or more but less than 15%
	1.6 for declarations less than 8%
	In case of deficiency —
	1.5 for declarations of 15% or more
	10% of the amount stated for declarations of 8% or more but less than 15%
	0.8 for declarations less than 8%
Phosphorus	If present in excess —
	3.6 for declarations of 16% or more
	22.5% of the amount stated for declarations of 12% or more but less than

Analytical constituents	Limits of variation (absolute value in percentage by weight, except where otherwise specified)
	16%
	2.7 for declarations of 6% or more but less than 12%
	45% of the amount stated for declarations of 1% or more but less than 6%
	0.45 for declarations less than 1%
	In case of deficiency —
	1.2 for declarations of 16% or more
	7.5% of the amount stated for declarations of 12% or more but less than 16%
	0.9 for declarations of 6% or more but less than 12%
	15% of the amount stated for declarations of 1% or more but less than 6%
	0.15 for declarations less than 1%
Potassium	If present in excess —
	4.5 for declarations of 15% or more
	30% of the amount stated for declarations of 7.5% or more but less than 15%
	2.25 for declarations of 5% or more but less than 7.5%
	45% of the amount stated for declarations of 0.7% or more but less than 5%
	0.3 for declarations less than 0.7%
	In case of deficiency —
	1.5 for declarations of 15% or more
	10% of the amount stated for declarations of 7.5% or more but less than 15%
	0.75 for declarations of 5% or more but less than 7.5%
	15% of the amount stated for declarations of 0.7% or more but less than 5%
	0.1 for declarations less than 0.7%
Protein	If present in excess —
	4 for declarations of 20% or more
	20% of the amount stated for declarations of 10% or more but less than 20%
	2 for declarations less than 10%
	In case of deficiency —
	2 for declarations of 20% or more
	10% of the amount stated for declarations of 10% or more but less than 20%
	1 for declarations less than 10%
Sodium	If present in excess —
	4.5 for declarations of 15% or more
	30% of the amount stated for declarations of 7.5% or more but less than 15%
	2.25 for declarations of 5% or more but less than 7.5%
	45% of the amount stated for declarations of 0.7% or more but less than 5%
	0.3 for declarations less than 0.7%

Analytical constituents	Limits of variation (absolute value in percentage by weight, except where otherwise specified)
	In case of deficiency — 1.5 for declarations of 15% or more 10% of the amount stated for declarations of 7.5% or more but less than 15% 0.75 for declarations of 5% or more but less than 7.5% 15% of the amount stated for declarations of 0.7% or more but less than 5% 0.1 for declarations less than 0.7%
Starch and total sugar plus starch	If present in excess — 5 for declarations of 25% or more 20% of the amount stated for declarations of 10% or more but less than 25% 2 for declarations less than 10% In case of deficiency — 2.5 for declarations of 25% or more 10% of the amount stated for declarations of 10% or more but less than 25% 1 for declarations less than 10%
Threonine	In case of deficiency — 30% of the amount stated
Total sugar	If present in excess — 4 for declarations of 20% or more 20% of the amount stated for declarations of 10% or more but less than 20% 2 for declarations less than 10% In case of deficiency — 2 for declarations of 20% or more 10% of the amount stated for declarations of 10% or more but less than 20% 1 for declarations less than 10%
Tryptophan	In case of deficiency — 30% of the amount stated

COMPOUND PET FOODS

Analytical constituents	Limits of variation (absolute value in percentage by weight, except where otherwise specified)
Ash	If present in excess — 1.5 for all declarations In the case of deficiency — 4.5 for all declarations
Ash insoluble in hydrochloric acid	If present in excess — 1.5 for all declarations
Calcium	If present in excess — 3.6 for declarations of 16% or more 22.5% of the amount stated for declarations of 12% or more but less than 16% 2.7 for declarations of 6% or more but less than 12% 45% of the amount stated for declarations of 1% or more but less than 6% 0.45 for declarations less than 1% In case of deficiency — 1.2 for declarations of 16% or more 7.5% of the amount stated for declarations of 12% or more but less than 16% 0.9 for declarations of 6% or more but less than 12% 15% of the amount stated for declarations of 1% or more but less than 6% 0.15 for declarations less than 1%
Cystine	In case of deficiency — 30% of the amount stated
Fibre	If present in excess — 1 for all declarations In case of deficiency — 3 for all declarations
Lysine	In case of deficiency — 30% of the amount stated
Magnesium	If present in excess — 4.5 for declarations of 15% or more 30% of the amount stated for declarations of 7.5% or more but less than 15% 2.25 for declarations of 5% or more but less than 7.5% 45% of the amount stated for declarations of 0.7% or more but less than 5% 0.3 for declarations less than 0.7% In case of deficiency —

Analytical constituents	Limits of variation (absolute value in percentage by weight, except where otherwise specified)
	1.5 for declarations of 15% or more
	10% of the amount stated for declarations of 7.5% or more but less than 15%
	0.75 for declarations of 5% or more but less than 7.5%
	15% of the amount stated for declarations of 0.7% or more but less than 5%
	0.1 for declarations less than 0.7%
Methionine	In case of deficiency —
	30% of the amount stated
Oils and fats	If present in excess —
	5 for all declarations
	In case of deficiency —
	2.5 for all declarations
Phosphorus	If present in excess —
	3.6 for declarations of 16% or more
	22.5% of the amount stated for declarations of 12% or more but less than 16%
	2.7 for declarations of 6% or more but less than 12%
	45% of the amount stated for declarations of 1% or more but less than 6%
	0.45 for declarations less than 1%
	In case of deficiency —
	1.2 for declarations of 16% or more
	7.5% of the amount stated for declarations of 12% or more but less than 16%
	0.9 for declarations of 6% or more but less than 12%
	15% of the amount stated for declarations of 1% or more but less than 6%
	0.15 for declarations less than 1%
Potassium	If present in excess —
	4.5 for declarations of 15% or more
	30% of the amount stated for declarations of 7.5% or more but less than 15%
	2.25 for declarations of 5% or more but less than 7.5%
	45% of the amount stated for declarations of 0.7% or more but less than 5%
	0.3 for declarations less than 0.7%
	In case of deficiency —
	1.5 for declarations of 15% or more
	10% of the amount stated for declarations of 7.5% or more but less than 15%
	0.75 for declarations of 5% or more but less than 7.5%
	15% of the amount stated for declarations of 0.7% or more but less than 5%
	0.1 for declarations less than 0.7%
Protein	If present in excess —
	6.4 for declarations of 20% or more

Analytical constituents	Limits of variation (absolute value in percentage by weight, except where otherwise specified)
	32% of the amount stated for declarations of 12.5% or more but less than 20%
	4 for declarations less than 12.5%
	In case of deficiency —
	3.2 for declarations of 20% or more
	16% of the amount stated for declarations of 12.5% or more but less than 20%
	2 for declarations less than 12.5%
Sodium	If present in excess —
	4.5 for declarations of 15% or more
	30% of the amount stated for declarations of 7.5% or more but less than 15%
	2.25 for declarations of 5% or more but less than 7.5%
	45% of the amount stated for declarations of 0.7% or more but less than 5%
	0.3 for declarations less than 0.7%
	In case of deficiency —
	1.5 for declarations of 15% or more
	10% of the amount stated for declarations of 7.5% or more but less than 15%
	0.75 for declarations of 5% or more but less than 7.5%
	15% of the amount stated for declarations of 0.7% or more but less than 5%
	0.1 for declarations less than 0.7%
Starch and total sugar plus starch	If present in excess —
	5 for declarations of 25% or more
	20% of the amount stated for declarations of 10% or more but less than 25%
	2 for declarations less than 10%
	In case of deficiency —
	2.5 for declarations of 25% or more
	10% of the amount stated for declarations of 10% or more but less than 25%
	1 for declarations less than 10%
Total sugar	If present in excess —
	4 for declarations of 20% or more
	20% of the amount stated for declarations of 10% or more but less than 20%
	2 for declarations less than 10%
	In case of deficiency —
	2 for declarations of 20% or more
	10% of the amount stated for declarations of 10% or more but less than 20%
	1 for declarations less than 10%
Threonine	In case of deficiency —
	30% of the amount stated

Analytical constituents	Limits of variation (absolute value in percentage by weight, except where otherwise specified)
Tryptophan	In case of deficiency — 30% of the amount stated

PART C

FEED MATERIALS

Analytical constituents	Limits of variation (absolute value in percentage by weight, except where otherwise specified)
Acid index	If present in excess — 1.5 for declarations of 15% or more 10% of the amount stated for declarations of 2% or more but less than 15% 0.2 for declarations less than 2%
Ash	If present in excess — 3 for declarations of 10% or more 30% of the amount stated for declarations of 5% or more but less than 10% 1.5 for declarations less than 5%
Ash insoluble in hydrochloric acid	If present in excess — 10% of the amount stated for declarations of 3% or more 0.3 for declarations less than 3%
Calcium	In case of deficiency — 1.5 for declarations of 15% or more 10% of the amount stated for declarations of 2% or more but less than 15% 0.2 for declarations less than 2%
Calcium carbonate	If present in excess — 1.5 for declarations of 15% or more 10% of the amount stated for declarations of 2% or more but less than 15% 0.2 for declarations less than 2%
Carotene	In case of deficiency — 30% of the amount stated
Chlorides expressed as NaCl	If present in excess — 10% of the amount stated for declarations of 3% or more 0.3 for declarations less than 3%
Fibre	If present in excess — 2.1 for declarations of 14% or more 15% of the amount stated for declarations of 6% or more but less than 14% 0.9 for declarations less than 6%
Inulin	In case of deficiency — 3 for declarations of 30% or more 10% of the amount stated for declarations of 10% or more but less than

Analytical constituents	Limits of variation (absolute value in percentage by weight, except where otherwise specified)
	30%
	1 for declarations less than 10%
Lysine	In case of deficiency —
	20% of the amount stated
Magnesium	In case of deficiency —
	1.5 for declarations of 15% or more
	10% of the amount stated for declarations of 2% or more but less than 15%
	0.2 for declarations less than 2%
Matter insoluble in light petroleum	If present in excess —
	1.5 for declarations of 15% or more
	10% of the amount stated for declarations of 2% or more but less than 15%
	0.2 for declarations less than 2%
Methionine	In case of deficiency —
	20% of the amount stated
Moisture	If present in excess —
	1 for declarations of 10% or more
	10% of the amount stated for declarations of 5% or more but less than 10%
	0.5 for declarations less than 5%
Oil and Fat	If present in excess —
	3.6 for declarations of 15% or more
	24% of the amount stated for declarations of 5% or more but less than 15%
	1.2 for declarations less than 5%
	In case of deficiency —
	1.8 for declarations of 15% or more
	12% of the amount stated for declarations of 5% or more but less than 15%
	0.6 for declarations less than 5%
Phosphorus	In case of deficiency —
	1.5 for declarations of 15% or more
	10% of the amount stated for declarations of 2% or more but less than 15%
	0.2 for declarations less than 2%
Protein	In case of deficiency —
	2 for declarations of 20% or more
	10% of the amount stated for declarations of 10% or more but less than 20%
	1 for declarations less than 10%
Protein equivalent of uric acid	If present in excess —

Analytical constituents	Limits of variation (absolute value in percentage by weight, except where otherwise specified)
	1.25, or 25% of the amount stated, whichever is the greater
Sodium	If present in excess — 4.5 for declarations of 15% or more 30% of the amount stated for declarations of 2% or more but less than 15% 0.6 for declarations less than 2%
Starch	In case of deficiency — 3 for declarations of 30% or more 10% of the amount stated for declarations of 10% or more but less than 30% 1 for declarations less than 10%
Sugar (total sugars, reducing sugars, sucrose, lactose, glucose (dextrose))	If present in excess — 4 for declarations of 20% or more 20% of the amount stated for declarations of 5% or more but less than 20% 1 for declarations less than 5% In case of deficiency — 2 for declarations of 20% or more 10% of the amount stated for declarations of 5% or more but less than 20% 0.5 for declarations less than 5%
Volatile nitrogenous bases	In case of deficiency — 20% of the amount stated
Xanthophyll	In case of deficiency — 30% of the amount stated

PART D

VITAMINS AND TRACE ELEMENTS

Vitamin/Trace Element	Limits of variation
Cobalt	± 50% of the amount stated
Copper	± 30% of the amount stated for declarations above 200 mg/kg ± 50% of the amount stated for declarations up to and including 200 mg/kg
Iodine	± 50% of the amount stated
Iron	± 30% of the amount stated for declarations of 250 mg/kg or more ± 50% of the amount stated for declarations less than 250 mg/kg

Vitamin/Trace Element	Limits of variation
Manganese	± 50% of the amount stated
Molybdenum	± 50% of the amount stated
Selenium	± 50% of the amount stated
Vitamins D_2 and D_3	± 30% of the amount stated for declarations above 4000 IU/kg ± 50% of the amount stated for declarations up to and including 4000 IU/kg
Vitamins other than D_2 and D_3	In case of deficiency — 30% of the amount stated
Zinc	± 50% of the amount stated

PART E

ENERGY VALUE OF COMPOUND FEEDING STUFFS

Feeding stuff	Limits of variation
Compound feeding stuffs for poultry	± 0.7 MJ/kg (absolute value)
Compound feeding stuffs for ruminants	± 7.5% of the amount stated
Compound feeding stuffs for pigs	± 7.5% of the amount stated
Feeding stuffs for particular nutritional purposes for cats and dogs	± 15% of the amount stated

PRESCRIBED LIMITS FOR UNDESIRABLE SUBSTANCES

Column 1 Undesirable substances	Column 2 Products intended for animal feed	Column 3 Maximum content in mg/kg of feeding stuffs referred to a moisture content of 12%
CHAPTER A		
Arsenic	Feed materials except:	2
	– meal made from grass, from dried lucerne and from dried clover and dried sugar beet pulp and dried molasses sugar beet pulp	4
	– palm kernel expeller	4 (of which the content of inorganic arsenic must be less than 2)
	– phosphates and calcareous marine algae	10
	– calcium carbonate	15
	– magnesium oxide	20
	– feedingstuff obtained from the processing of fish or other marine animals	15 (of which the content of inorganic arsenic must be less than 2)
	– seaweed meal and feed materials derived from seaweed	40 (of which the content of inorganic arsenic must be less than 2)
	Complete feeding stuffs except:	2
	– complete feeding stuffs for fish and fur–producing animals	6 (of which the content of inorganic arsenic must be less than 2)
	Complementary feeding stuffs except:	4
	– mineral feeding stuffs	12
		Note in respect of all entries in column 3 The maximum levels refer to total arsenic
Cadmium	Feed materials of vegetable origin	1
	Feed materials of animal origin (with the exception of feeding stuffs for pets)	2
	Phosphates	10
	Complete feeding stuffs for cattle, sheep and goats (with the exception of complete feeding stuffs for calves, lambs and kids)	1
	Other complete feeding stuffs (with the exception of feeding stuffs for pets)	0.5

Column 1 Undesirable substances	Column 2 Products intended for animal feed	Column 3 Maximum content in mg/kg of feeding stuffs referred to a moisture content of 12%
CHAPTER A		
	Mineral feeding stuffs	5
	Other complementary feeding stuffs for cattle, sheep and goats	0.5
Dioxin (sum of polychlorinated dibenzo–para–dioxins (PCDDs) and polychlorinated dibenzo–furans (PCDFs) expressed in World Health Organisation (WHO) toxic equivalents, using the WHO–TEFs (toxic equivalency factors, 1997))	All feed materials of plant origin including vegetable oils and by–products	0.75 ng WHO–PCDD/F–TEQ/kg
	Minerals as listed in Section 11 of Part II of Schedule 2	1.0 ng WHO–PCDD/F–TEQ/kg
	Kaolinitic clay, calcium sulphate dihydrate, vermiculite, natrolite–phonolite, synthetic calcium aluminates and clinoptilolite of sedimentary origin belonging to the group "binders, anti–caking agents and coagulants" authorised under the Additives Directive or the Additives Regulation	0.75 ng WHO–PCDD/F–TEQ/kg
	Animal fat, including milk fat and egg fat	2.0 ng WHO–PCDD/F–TEQ/kg
	Other land animal products including milk and milk products and eggs and egg products	0.75 ng WHO–PCDD/F–TEQ/kg
	Fish oil	6 ng WHO–PCDD/F–TEQ/kg
	Fish, other aquatic animals, their products and by–products with the exception of fish oil and fish protein hydrolysates containing more than 20% fat	1.25 ng WHO–PCDD/F–TEQ/kg
	Compound feedingstuffs, with the exception of feedingstuffs for fur animals, pet foods and feedingstuffs for fish	0.75 ng WHO–PCDD/F–TEQ/kg
	Feedingstuffs for fish and pet foods	2.25 ng WHO–PCDD/F–TEQ/kg
	Fish protein hydrolysates containing more than 20% fat	2.25 ng WHO–PCDD/F–TEQ/kg
	Note in respect of the entry in Column 2 relating to fish, other aquatic	**Note in respect of all the entries in Column 3**

Column 1 Undesirable substances	Column 2 Products intended for animal feed	Column 3 Maximum content in mg/kg of feeding stuffs referred to a moisture content of 12%
CHAPTER A		
	animals, their products and by-products with the exception of fish oil and fish protein hydrolysates containing more than 20% fat Fresh fish directly delivered and used without intermediate processing for the production of feedingstuffs for fur animals is exempted from the maximum limit and a maximum level of 4.0 ng WHO–PCDD/F–TEQ/kg product is applicable to fresh fish used for the direct feeding of pet animals, zoo and circus animals. The products, processed animal proteins produced from these animals (fur animals, pet animals, zoo and circus animals) cannot enter the food chain and the feeding thereof is prohibited to farmed animals which are kept, fattened or bred for the production of food.	Upper–bound concentrations; upper–bound concentrations are calculated assuming that all values of the different congeners less than the limit of quantification are equal to the limit of quantification
Fluorine	Feed materials except:	150
	– feedingstuffs of animal origin with the exception of marine crustaceans such as marine krill	500
	– phosphates and marine crustaceans such as marine krill	2000
	– calcium carbonate	350
	– magnesium oxide	600
	– calcareous marine algae	1000
	Complete feeding stuffs except:	150
	– complete feeding stuffs for cattle, sheep and goats	
	– in milk	30
	– other	50
	– complete feeding stuffs for pigs	100
	– complete feeding stuffs for poultry	350
	– complete feeding stuffs for chicks	250
	Mineral mixtures for cattle, sheep and goats	2000
	Other complementary feeding stuffs	125 (fluorine content per percentage point phosphorus in the feeding stuff)
Lead	Feed materials except:	10
	– grass meal, lucerne meal or clover	40

54

Column 1 Undesirable substances	Column 2 Products intended for animal feed	Column 3 Maximum content in mg/kg of feeding stuffs referred to a moisture content of 12%
CHAPTER A		
	meal	
	– calcium carbonate	20
	– phosphates and calcareous marine algae	15
	– yeast	5
	Complete feeding stuffs	5
	Complementary feeding stuffs except:	10
	– mineral feeding stuffs	15
Mercury	Feed materials except:	0.1
	– feed materials produced by the processing of fish or other marine animals	0.5
	Complete feeding stuffs except:	0.1
	– complete feeding stuffs for dogs or cats	0.4
	Complementary feeding stuffs (with the exception of complementary feeding stuffs for dogs and cats)	0.2
Nitrites	Fish meal	60 (expressed as sodium nitrite)
	Complete feeding stuffs except feeding stuffs intended for pets other than birds and aquarium fish	15 (expressed as sodium nitrite)

Column 1 Undesirable substances	Column 2 Products intended for animal feed	Column 3 Maximum content in mg/kg of feeding stuffs referred to a moisture content of 12%
CHAPTER B		
Aflatoxin B$_1$	All feed materials	0.02
	Complete feeding stuffs for cattle, sheep and goats except:	0.02
	– dairy animals	0.005
	– calves and lambs	0.01
	Complete feeding stuffs for pigs and poultry (except piglets and chicks)	0.02
	Other complete feeding stuffs	0.01
	Complementary feeding stuffs for cattle, sheep and goats (except complementary feeding stuffs for dairy animals, calves and lambs)	0.02
	Complementary feeding stuffs for pigs and poultry (except piglets and chicks)	0.02
	Other complementary feeding stuffs	0.005
Castor oil plant *Ricinus communis* L.	All feeding stuffs	10 (expressed in terms of castor oil plant husks)
Crotalaria spp.	All feeding stuffs	100
Free Gossypol	Feed materials except:	20
	– cotton–seed	5000
	– cotton–seed cakes	1200
	Complete feeding stuffs except:	20
	– complete feeding stuffs for cattle, sheep and goats	500
	– complete feeding stuffs for poultry (except laying hens) and calves	100
	– complete feeding stuffs for rabbits and pigs (except piglets)	60
Hydrocyanic acid	Feed materials except:	50
	– linseed	250
	– linseed cakes	350
	– manioc products and almond cakes	100
	Complete feeding stuffs except:	50
	– complete feeding stuffs for chicks	10
Rye Ergot *Claviceps purpurea*	All feeding stuffs containing unground cereals	1000

Column 1 Undesirable substances	Column 2 Products intended for animal feed	Column 3 Maximum content in mg/kg of feeding stuffs referred to a moisture content of 12%
CHAPTER C		
Apricots – *Prunus armeniaca* L.	}	{
Bitter almond – *Prunus dulcis* (Mill.) D.A.Webb var. *amara* (DC.) Focke (= *Prunus amygdalus* Batsch var. *amara* (DC.) Focke)	}	{
Unhusked beech mast – *Fagus silvatica* (L.) Camelina–*Camelina sativa* (L.) Cranz	}	{
Mowrah, bassia, madhuca – *Madhuca longifolia* (L.) Macbr. (= *Bassia longifolia* L = *Illipe malabrorum* Engl.) *Madhuca indica* Gmelin. (= *Bassia latifolia* (Rosch.) F. Mueller)	}	{ Seeds and fruits of the plant species listed opposite as well as their processed derivatives may only be present in feeding stuffs in trace amounts not quantitatively determinable
Purghera – *Jatropha curcas* L.	} All feeding stuffs	{
Croton – *Croton tiglium* L. Indian mustard – *Brassica juncea* (L.) Czern. and Coss. ssp. *integrifolia* (West.) Thell	}	{
Sareptian mustard – *Brassica juncea* (L.) Czern. and Coss. ssp. *juncea*	}	{
Chinese mustard – *Brassica juncea* (L.) Czern. and Coss. ssp. *juncea* var. *lutea* Batalin	}	{
Black mustard – *Brassica nigra* (L.) Koch	}	{
Ethiopian mustard – *Brassica carinata* A Braun	}	{
Theobromine	Complete feeding stuffs	300

	except: – complete feeding stuffs for adult cattle	700
Vinylthiooxazolidone (*Vinyloxyzolidine thione*)	Complete feeding stuffs for poultry	1000
	except: – complete feeding stuffs for laying hens	500
Volatile mustard oil	Feed materials except:	100
	– rape–seed cakes	4000 (expressed as allyl isothiocyanate)
	Complete feeding stuffs	150 (expressed as allyl isothiocyanate)
	except: – complete feeding stuffs for cattle, sheep and goats (except calves, lambs and kids)	1000 (expressed as allyl isothiocyanate)
	– complete feeding stuffs for pigs (except piglets) and poultry	500 (expressed as allyl isothiocyanate)
Weed seeds and unground and uncrushed fruit containing alkaloids, glucosides or other toxic substances separately or in combination including:	All feeding stuffs	3000
(a) *Lolium temulentum* L.		1000
(b) *Lolium remotum* Schrank		1000
(c) *Datura stramonium* L.		1000

Column 1 *Undesirable substances*			Column 2 *Products intended for animal feed*	Column 3 *Maximum content in mg/kg feeding stuffs referred to a moisture content of 12%*
CHAPTER D				
Aldrin Dieldrin	} singly, or } combined } expressed as } dieldrin		All feeding stuffs except fats	0.01 0.2
Camphechlor (Toxaphene)			All feeding stuffs	0.1
Chlordane (sum of cis– and trans–isomers and of oxychlordane, expressed as Chlordane)			All feeding stuffs except fats	0.02 0.05
DDT (sum of DDT, TDE and DDE isomers, expressed as DDT)			All feeding stuffs except fats	0.05 0.5
Endosulphan (sum of alpha- and beta-isomers and of endosulphan sulphate, expressed as endosulphan)			All feeding stuffs except – maize and the products derived from the processing thereof – oilseeds and the products derived from the processing thereof – complete feeding stuffs for fish	0.1 0.2 0.5 0.005
Endrin (sum of endrin and delta–keto–endrin, expressed as endrin)			All feeding stuffs except fats	0.01 0.05
Heptachlor (sum of heptachlor and of heptachlor–epoxide, expressed as heptachlor			All feeding stuffs except fats	0.01 0.2
Hexachlorobenzene (HCB)			All feeding stuffs except fats	0.01 0.2
Hexachlorocyclohexane (HCH) – alpha–isomers – beta–isomers			All feed stuffs except fats Feed materials except fats Compound feeding stuffs except	0.02 0.2 0.01 0.1 0.01

Column 1 Undesirable substances		Column 2 Products intended for animal feed	Column 3 Maximum content in mg/kg feeding stuffs referred to a moisture content of 12%
CHAPTER D			
		compound feeding stuffs for dairy cattle	0.005
– gamma–isomers		All feeding stuffs except fats	0.2 2.0

SCHEDULE 6

CONTROL OF CERTAIN PROTEIN SOURCES

		Column 1 *Name of product group*	Column 2 *Permitted products*		Column 3 *Designation of nutritive principle or identity of micro—organisms*	Column 4 *Culture substrate (specifications, if any)*	Column 5[1] *Composition characteristics of product*	Column 6 *Animal species*	Column 7[1] *Name of product and specified particulars*
1.		Proteins obtained from the following groups of micro—organisms							
1.1		*Bacteria*							
1.1.1.		Bacteria cultivated on methanol	Protein product of fermentation obtained by culture of *Methylophilus methylotrophus* on methanol	1.1.1.1.	*Methylophilus methylotrophus NCIB* strain 10.515	Methanol	protein: min 68%— Reflectance index: at least 50	Pigs, calves, poultry and fish	Declarations to be made on the label or packaging of the product: – name of the product; — protein; – ash; – fat; – moisture content; – instructions for use; – "avoid inhalation"; ... approval number Declarations to be made on the label or the packaging of compound feeding stuffs: – amount of the product contained in the feeding stuff

		Column 2 Permitted products	Column 3 Designation of nutritive principle or identity of micro-organisms	Column 4 Culture substrate (specifications, if any)	Column 5[(1)] Composition characteristics of product	Column 6 Animal species	Column 7[(1)] Name of product and specified particulars
Column 1 Name of product group							
1.1.2.	Bacteria cultivated on natural gas	1.1.2.1.	Protein product of fermentation from natural gas obtained by culture of:	*Methyloccus capsulatus (Bath)* NCIMB strain 11132 *Alcaligenes acidovorans* NCIMB strain 12387 *Bacillus brevis* NCIMB strain 13288	Natural gas: (approx. 91% methane, 5% ethane, 2% propane, 0.5% isobutane, 0.5% n–butane, 1% other components).	protein: min 65%	– Pigs for fattening from 25 to 60 kg – Calves from 80 kg on – Salmon	Declarations to be made on the label or the packaging of the product: — the name "Protein product of fermentation from natural gas obtained by culture of *Methylococcus capsulatus (Bath)*, *Alcaligenes acidovorans*, *Bacillus brevis* and *Bacillus firmus*" –– protein –– ash –– fat –– moisture content
			Methylococcus capsulatus (Bath) *Alcaligenes acidovorans*, *Bacillus brevis* and *Bacillus firmus*, and the cells of which have been killed	*Bacillus firmus* NCIMB strain 13280	ammonia, mineral salts			–– instructions for use maximum incorporation rate in the feed: – 8% pigs for fattening – 8% calves – 19% salmon (freshwater) – 33% salmon (seawater) "avoid inhalation"; Declarations to be made on the label or packaging of the compound feedingstuffs: — the name "Protein product obtained by bacterial fermentation of natural gas" — amount of the product contained in the feedingstuff — approval number
1.2.	*Yeasts*						

Column 1 Name of product group		Column 2 Permitted products	Column 3 Designation of nutritive principle or identity of micro-organisms	Column 4 Culture substrate (specifications, if any)	Column 5[(1)] Composition characteristics of product	Column 6 Animal species	Column 7[(1)] Name of product and specified particulars
1.2.1.	Yeasts cultivated on substrates of animal or vegetable origin	– Yeasts obtained from the micro-organisms and substrates listed in columns 3 and 4 respectively, the cells of which have been killed	} Saccharomyces cerevisiae } Saccharomyces carlshergiensis } Kluyveromyces lactis } Kluyveromyces fragilis } Candida guilliermondii	Molasses, distillery residues, cereals and products containing starch, fruit juice, whey, lactic acid, hydrolized vegetable fibres	In relation to Candida guilliermondii only, a minimum dry matter content of 16% applies	All animal species, except in the case of Candida guilliermondii which is only authorised for pigs for fattening	
1.2.2.	Yeasts cultivated on substrates other than those given in 1.2.1.						
1.3.	Algae						
1.4.	Lower fungi						

63

Column 1 Name of product group		Column 2 Permitted products	Column 3 Designation of nutritive principle or identity of micro-organisms	Column 4 Culture substrate (specifications, if any)	Column 5[(1)] Composition characteristics of product	Column 6 Animal species	Column 7[(1)] Name of product and specified particulars
1.4.1.	Products from production of antibiotics by fermentation						
		1.4.1.1. Mycelium, wet by-product from the production of penicillin, ensiled by means of *lactobacillus brevis, plantarum, sake, collenoid* and *streptococcus lactis* to inactivate the penicillin, and heat treated	Nitrogenous compound Penicillium chrysogenum *ATCC 48271*	Different sources of carbohydrates and their hydrolysates	Nitrogen expressed as protein: min 7%	Ruminants and pigs	Declarations to be made on the label or packaging of the product: — the name "Mycelium silage from the production of penicillin"; — nitrogen expressed as protein; — ash; — moisture; — animal species or category; — approval number; Declaration to be made on the label or packaging of the compound feeding stuff: - in the name "Mycelium silage from the production of penicillin"
2.	Non-protein nitrogenous compounds						
2.1.	Ammonium salts	2.1.1. Ammonium lactate, produced by fermentation with *Lactobacillus bulgaricus*	$CH_3CHOHCOONH_4$	Whey	Nitrogen expressed as protein: min 44%	Ruminants from the beginning of rumination	Declarations to be made on the label or packaging of the product: — the name "Ammonium lactate from fermentation"; - ash — moisture; — animal species or category; Declarations to be made on the label or packaging of compound feeding stuffs:

Column 1 Name of product group		Column 2 Permitted products	Column 3 Designation of nutritive principle or identity of micro-organisms	Column 4 Culture substrate (specifications, if any)	Column 5[1] Composition characteristics of product	Column 6 Animal species	Column 7[1] Name of product and specified particulars
							– the name "Ammonium lactate from fermentation; – amount of product contained in the feeding stuff; – percentage of the total protein provided by non-protein nitrogen; – indication, in the instructions for use, of the level of total non–protein nitrogen which should not be exceeded in the daily ration of each animal species or category
	2.1.2.	Ammonium acetate in aqueous solution	CH$_3$COONH$_4$		Ammonium acetate: min 55%	Ruminants from the start of rumination	Declarations to be made on the label or packaging of the product: – the words "Ammonium acetate"; – nitrogen content; – moisture content; – animal species or category; Declarations to be made on the label or packaging of compound feeding stuffs; – the words "Ammonium acetate"; – the amount of the product contained in the feeding stuffs; – percentage of the total protein provided by non–protein nitrogen; – indication in the instructions for use of the level of total non–protein nitrogen which should not be exceeded in the daily ration for each animal species or category

Column 1 *Name of product group*		Column 2 *Permitted products*	Column 3 *Designation of nutritive principle or identity of micro—organisms*	Column 4 *Culture substrate (specifications, if any)*	Column 5[1] *Composition characteristics of product*	Column 6 *Animal species*	Column 7[1] *Name of product and specified particulars*
	2.1.3.	Ammonium sulphate in aqueous solution	$(NH_4)_2SO_4$		Ammonium sulphate: min 35%	Ruminants from the start of rumination	Declarations to be made on the label or packaging of the product: – the words "Ammonium sulphate"; – nitrogen and moisture contents; – animal species; – in the case of young ruminants, the incorporation rate in the daily ration may not exceed 0.5%; Declarations to be made on the label or packaging of compound feeding stuffs: – the words "Ammonium sulphate"; – the amount of the product contained in the feeding stuff; – percentage of the total protein provided by non—protein nitrogen; – indication in the instructions for use of the level of total non—protein nitrogen which should not be exceeded in the daily ration of each animal species; – in the case of young ruminants, the incorporation rate in the daily ration may not exceed 0.5%

[1] In this Schedule the contents laid down or to be declared in accordance with Columns 5 and 7 refer to the product as such.

SCHEDULE 7   Regulation 19 and Schedule 3 Part I, paragraphs 18, 25 and 30

PERMITTED FEEDING STUFFS INTENDED FOR PARTICULAR NUTRITIONAL PURPOSES AND PROVISIONS RELATING TO THEIR USE

CHAPTER A

Column 1 Particular nutritional purpose	Column 2 Essential nutritional characteristics	Column 3 Species or category of animal	Column 4 Labelling declarations	Column 5 Recommended length of time for use	Column 6 Other provisions
Support of renal function in case of chronic renal insufficiency[1]	Low level of phosphorus and restricted level of protein but of high quality	Dogs and cats	— Protein source(s) — Calcium — Phosphorus — Potassium — Sodium — Contents of essential fatty acids (if added)	Initially up to 6 months[2]	Indicate on the package, container or label: "It is recommended that a veterinarian's opinion be sought before use or before extending the period of use." Indicate in the instructions for use: "Water should be available at all times."
Dissolution of struvite stones[3]	- Urine acidifying properties, low level of magnesium, and restricted level of protein but of high quality	Dogs	— Protein source(s) — Calcium — Phosphorus — Sodium — Magnesium — Potassium — Chlorides — Sulphur — Urine acidifying substances	5 to 12 weeks	Indicate on the package, container or label: "It is recommended that a veterinarian's opinion be sought before use." Indicate in the instructions for use: "Water should be available at all times."
	– Urine acidifying properties and low level of magnesium	Cats	– Calcium – Phosphorus – Sodium		

Column 1 Particular nutritional purpose	Column 2 Essential nutritional characteristics	Column 3 Species or category of animal	Column 4 Labelling declarations	Column 5 Recommended length of time for use	Column 6 Other provisions
			– Magnesium – Potassium – Chlorides – Sulphur – Total taurine – Urine acidifying substances		
Reduction of struvite stone recurrence[4]	– Urine acidifying properties and moderate level of magnesium	Dogs and cats	– Calcium – Phosphorus – Sodium – Magnesium – Potassium – Chlorides – Sulphur – Urine acidifying substances	Up to 6 months	Indicate on the package, container or label: "It is recommended that a veterinarian's opinion be sought before use."
Reduction of urate stones formation	Low level of purines, low level of protein but of high quality	Dogs and cats	– Protein source(s)	Up to 6 months but lifetime use in cases of irreversible disturbance of uric acid metabolism	Indicate on the package, container or label: "It is recommended that a veterinarian's opinion be sought before use."
Reduction of oxalate stones formation	Low level of calcium, low level of Vitamin D, and urine alkalising properties	Dogs and cats	– Phosphorus – Calcium – Sodium – Magnesium – Potassium – Chlorides – Sulphur – Total Vitamin D – Hydroxyproline – Urine alkalising substances	Up to 6 months	Indicate on the package, container or label: "It is recommended that a veterinarian's opinion be sought before use."

Column 1 Particular nutritional purpose	Column 2 Essential nutritional characteristics	Column 3 Species or category of animal	Column 4 Labelling declarations	Column 5 Recommended length of time for use	Column 6 Other provisions
Reduction of cystine stones formation	Low level of protein, moderate level of sulphur amino acids and urine alkalising properties	Dogs and cats	– Total sulphur amino acids – Sodium – Potassium – Chlorides – Sulphur – Urine acidifying substances	Initially up to 1 year	Indicate on the package, container or label: "It is recommended that a veterinarian's opinion be sought before use or before extending the period of use."
Reduction of feed material and nutrient intolerances [5]	Selected protein source(s) and/or Selected carbohydrate source(s)	Dogs and cats	– Protein source(s) – Content of essential fatty acids (if added) – Carbohydrate source(s) – Contents of essential fatty acids (if added)	3 to 8 weeks; if signs of intolerance disappear this feed can be used indefinitely	...
Reduction of acute intestinal absorptive disorders	Increased level of electrolytes and highly digestible feed materials	Dogs and cats	– Highly digestible feed materials including their treatment if appropriate – Sodium – Potassium – Source(s) of mucilaginous substances (if added)	1 to 2 weeks	Indicate on the package, container or label: "During periods of and recovery from acute diarrhoea." "It is recommended that a veterinarian's opinion be sought before use."
Compensation for maldigestion [6]	Highly digestible feed materials and low level of fat	Dogs and cats	– Highly digestible feed materials including their treatment if appropriate	3 to 12 weeks, but lifetime in case of chronic pancreatic insufficiency	Indicate on the package, container or label: "It is recommended that a veterinarian's opinion be sought before use."
Support of heart function in case of chronic cardiac insufficiency	Low level of sodium and increased K/Na ratio	Dogs and cats	– Sodium – Potassium – Magnesium	Initially up to 6 months	Indicate on the package, container or label: "It is recommended that a veterinarian's opinion be sought before use or before extending the period of use."

Column 1 Particular nutritional purpose	Column 2 Essential nutritional characteristics	Column 3 Species or category of animal	Column 4 Labelling declarations	Column 5 Recommended length of time for use	Column 6 Other provisions
Regulation of glucose supply (Diabetes mellitus)	Low level of rapid glucose-releasing carbohydrates	Dogs and cats	— Carbohydrate source(s) — Treatment of carbohydrates if appropriate – Starch – Total sugar — Fructose (if added) — Content of essential fatty acids (if added) – Source(s) of short and medium chain fatty acids (if added)	Initially up to 6 months	Indicate on the package, container or label: "It is recommended that a veterinarian's opinion be sought before use or before extending the period of use."
Support of liver function in case of chronic liver insufficiency	High quality protein, moderate level of protein, high level of essential fatty acids and high level of highly digestive carbohydrates	Dogs	– Protein source(s) – Content of essential fatty acids – Highly digestible carbohydrates including their treatment if appropriate – Sodium – Total copper	Initially up to 6 months	Indicate on the package, container or label: "It is recommended that a veterinarian's opinion be sought before use or before extending the period of use." Indicate in the instructions for use: "Water should be available at all times".
Support of liver function in case of chronic liver insufficiency	High quality protein, moderate level of protein and high level of essential fatty acids	Cats	– Protein source(s) – Content of essential fatty acids – Sodium – Total copper	Initially up to 6 months	Indicate on the package, container or label: "It is recommended that a veterinarian's opinion be sought before use or before extending the period of use." Indicate in the instructions for use: "Water should be available at all times".
Regulation of lipid metabolism in case of hyperlipidaemia	Low level of fat and high level of essential fatty acids	Dogs and cats	— Content of essential fatty acids —Contents of n–3 fatty acids (if added)	Initially up to 2 months	Indicate on the package, container or label: "It is recommended that a veterinarian's opinion be sought before use or before extending the period of use."

Column 1 Particular nutritional purpose	Column 2 Essential nutritional characteristics	Column 3 Species or category of animal	Column 4 Labelling declarations	Column 5 Recommended length of time for use	Column 6 Other provisions
Reduction of copper in the liver	Low level of copper	Dogs	– Total copper	Initially up to 6 months	Indicate on the package, container or label: "It is recommended that a veterinarian's opinion be sought before use or before extending the period of use."
Reduction of excessive body weight	Low energy density	Dogs and cats	– Energy value	Until target body weight is achieved	In the instructions for use an appropriate daily intake must be recommended
Nutritional restoration, convalescence[7]	High energy density, high concentration of essential nutrients and highly digestible feed materials	Dogs and cats	– Highly digestible feed materials including their treatment if appropriate – Energy value – Contents of n–3 and n–6 fatty acids (if added)	Until restoration is achieved	In the case of feeding stuffs specially presented to be given via tubing, indicate on the package, container or label: "Administration under veterinary supervision."
Support of skin function in case of dermatosis and excessive loss of hair	High level of essential fatty acids	Dogs and cats	– Contents of essential fatty acids	Up to 2 months	Indicate on the package, container or label: "It is recommended that a veterinarian's opinion be sought before use."
Reduction of the risk of milk fever	– Low level of calcium and/or – Low cations/anions ratio	Dairy cows	– Calcium – Phosphorus – Magnesium – Calcium – Phosphorus – Sodium – Potassium – Chlorides – Sulphur	1 to 4 weeks before calving	Indicate in the instructions for use: "Stop feeding after calving."
Reduction of the risk of ketosis[8]	Feed materials providing glucogenic energy sources	Dairy cows and ewes	– Feed materials providing glucogenic energy sources – Propane–1, 2–diol (if added as a glucose precursor) – Glycerol (if added as a glucose precursor)	3 to 6 weeks after calving[9]. Last 6 weeks before and the first 3 weeks after lambing[10]	

Column 1 Particular nutritional purpose	Column 2 Essential nutritional characteristics	Column 3 Species or category of animal	Column 4 Labelling declarations	Column 5 Recommended length of time for use	Column 6 Other provisions
Reduction of the risk of tetany (hypomagnesaemia)	High level of magnesium, easily available carbohydrates, moderate level of protein and low level of potassium	Ruminants	– Starch – Total sugars – Magnesium – Sodium – Potassium	3 to 10 weeks during periods of fast grass growth	In the instructions for use guidance shall be provided on the balance of the daily ration, with regard to the inclusion of fibre and easily available energy sources. In the case of feeding stuffs for ovines indicate on the package, container or label: "Especially for lactating ewes."
Reduction of the risk of acidosis	Low level of easily fermentable carbohydrates and high buffering capacity	Ruminants	– Starch – Total sugars	Maximum 2 months[11]	In the instructions for use guidance shall be provided on the balance of the daily ration, with regard to the inclusion of fibre and easily fermentable carbohydrate sources. In the case of feeding stuffs for dairy cows indicate on the package, container or label: "Especially for high yielding cows." In the case of feeding stuffs for ruminants for fattening indicate on the package, container or label: "Especially for intensively fed ....."[12]
Stabilisation of water and electrolyte balance	Predominantly electrolytes and easily absorbable carbohydrates	Calves Piglets Lambs Kids Foals	– Carbohydrate source(s) – Sodium – Potassium – Chlorides	1 to 7 days (1 to 3 days if fed exclusively)	Indicate on the package, container or label: "In case of risk of, during periods of, or recovery from digestive disturbance (diarrhoea). It is recommended that a veterinarian's opinion be sought before use."

Column 1 Particular nutritional purpose	Column 2 Essential nutritional characteristics	Column 3 Species or category of animal	Column 4 Labelling declarations	Column 5 Recommended length of time for use	Column 6 Other provisions
Reduction of the risk of urinary calculi	Low level of phosphorus, magnesium and urine acidifying properties	Ruminants	— Calcium — Phosphorus — Sodium — Magnesium — Potassium — Chlorides — Sulphur — Urine acidifying substances	Up to 6 weeks	Indicate on the package, container or label: "Especially for intensively fed young animals." Indicate in the instructions for use: "Water should be available at all times."
Reduction of stress reactions	High level of magnesium and/or highly digestible feed materials	Pigs	— Magnesium — Highly digestible feed materials including their treatment if appropriate; — Contents of n–3 fatty acids (if added)	1 to 7 days	Guidance shall be provided on the situation in which the use of this feed is appropriate.
Stabilisation of physiological digestion	Low buffering capacity and highly digestible feed materials	Piglets	— Highly digestible feed materials including their treatment if appropriate — Buffering capacity — Source(s) of astringent substances (if added) — Source(s) of mucilaginuous substances (if added)	2 to 4 weeks	Indicate on the package, container or label: "In the case of risk of, during periods of, or recovery from, digestive disturbance."
	Highly digestible feed materials	Pigs	— Highly digestible feed materials including their treatment if appropriate — Source(s) of astringent substances (if added) — Source(s) of mucilaginous substances (if added)		

73

Column 1 Particular nutritional purpose	Column 2 Essential nutritional characteristics	Column 3 Species or category of animal	Column 4 Labelling declarations	Column 5 Recommended length of time for use	Column 6 Other provisions
Reduction of the risk of constipation	Feed materials stimulating intestinal passage	Sows	— Feed materials stimulating intestinal passage	10 to 14 days before and 10 to 14 days after farrowing	
Reduction of the risk of fatty liver syndrome	Low energy and high proportion of metabolizable energy from lipids with high level of polyunsaturated fatty acids	Laying hens	— Energy value (calculated according to EEC method – see Schedule 1) — Percentage of metabolizable energy from lipids — Content of polyunsaturated fatty acids	Up to 12 weeks	
Compensation for malabsorption	Low level of saturated fatty acids and high level of fat soluble vitamins	Poultry excluding geese and pigeons	— Percentage of saturated fatty acids in relation to total fatty acids — Total vitamin A — Total vitamin D — Total vitamin E — Total vitamin K	During the first 2 weeks after hatching	
Compensation for chronic insufficiency of small intestine function	Highly precaecally digestible carbohydrates, proteins and fats	Equines[13]	— Source(s) of highly digestible carbohydrates, proteins and fats including their treatment if appropriate	Initially up to 6 months	Guidance should be provided on the situations in which the use of this feed is appropriate and the manner in which it should be fed including many small meals per day. Indicate on the package, container or label: "It is recommended that a veterinarian's opinion be sought before use or before extending the period of use."
Compensation of chronic digestive disorders of large intestine	Highly digestible fibre	Equines	— Fibre source(s) — Contents of n–3 fatty acids (if added)	Initially up to 6 months	Guidance should be provided on the situations in which the use of the feed is appropriate and the manner in which the feed should be fed.

Column 1 Particular nutritional purpose	Column 2 Essential nutritional characteristics	Column 3 Species or category of animal	Column 4 Labelling declarations	Column 5 Recommended length of time for use	Column 6 Other provisions
					Indicate on the package, container or label: "It is recommended that a veterinarian's opinion be sought before use or before extending the period of use."
Reduction of stress reactions	Highly digestible feed materials	Equines	– Magnesium – Highly digestible feed materials including their treatment if appropriate – Content of n–3 fatty acids (if added)	2 to 4 weeks	Guidance shall be provided on the precise situations in which the use of the feed is appropriate.
Compensation of electrolyte loss in cases of heavy sweating	Predominantly electrolytes and easily absorbable carbohydrates	Equines	– Calcium – Sodium – Magnesium – Potassium – Chlorides – Glucose	1 to 3 days	Guidance shall be provided on the precise situations in which the use of the feed is appropriate. When the feed corresponds to a significant part of the daily ration, guidance should be provided to prevent the risk of abrupt changes in the nature of the feed. Indicate on the instructions for use: "Water should be available at all times."
Nutritional restoration, convalescence	High concentration of essential nutrients and highly digestible feed materials	Equines	– Highly digestible feed materials including their treatment if appropriate – Content of n–3 and n–6 fatty acids (if added)	Until restoration is achieved	Guidance shall be provided on the situations in which the use of this feed is appropriate. In the case of feeding stuffs specially presented to be given via tubing, indicate on the package, container or label: "Administration under veterinary supervision."

Column 1 Particular nutritional purpose	Column 2 Essential nutritional characteristics	Column 3 Species or category of animal	Column 4 Labelling declarations	Column 5 Recommended length of time for use	Column 6 Other provisions
Support of liver function in case of chronic liver insufficiency	Low level of protein but of high quality and highly digestible carbohydrates	Equines	– Protein and fibre source(s) – Highly digestible carbohydrates including their treatment if appropriate – Methionine – Choline – Contents of n-3 fatty acids (if added)	Initially up to 6 months	Guidance should be provided on the manner in which the feed should be fed including many small meals per day. Indicate on the package, container or label: "It is recommended that a veterinarian's opinion be sought before use or before extending the period of use."
Support of renal function in case of chronic renal insufficiency	Low level of protein but of high quality and low level of phosphorus	Equines	– Protein source(s) – Calcium – Phosphorus – Potassium – Magnesium – Sodium	Initially up to 6 months	Indicate on the package, container or label: "It is recommended that a veterinarian's opinion be sought before use or before extending the period of use." Indicate on the instructions for use: "Water should be available at all times."

(1) If appropriate the manufacturer may also recommend use for temporary renal insufficiency.

(2) If the feeding stuff is recommended for temporary renal insufficiency the recommended period for use shall be two to four weeks.

(3) In the case of feeding stuffs for cats, "feline lower urinary tract disease" or "feline urological syndrome – F.U.S." may complete the particular nutritional purpose.

(4) In the case of feeding stuffs for cats, "feline lower urinary tract disease" or "feline urological syndrome – F.U.S." may complete the particular nutritional purpose.

(5) In the case of feeding stuffs for a particular intolerance reference to the specific intolerance can replace "feed material and nutrient."

(6) The manufacturer may complete the particular nutritional purpose with the reference "exocrine pancreatic insufficiency."

(7) In the case of feeding stuffs for cats, the manufacturer may complete the particular nutritional purpose with a reference to "Feline hepatic lipidosis."

(8) The term "ketosis" may be replaced by "acetonaemia". The manufacturers may also recommend the use of ketosis recuperation.

(9) In the case of feeding stuffs for dairy cows.

(10) In the case of feeding stuffs for ewes.

(11) In the case of feeding stuffs for dairy cows, "maximum two months from the start of lactation."

(12) Indicate the category of ruminants concerned.

(13) In the case of feeding stuffs specially prepared to meet the specific conditions of very old animals (easily digestible feed materials) a reference to "old animals" shall complete the indication of the species or category of animal.

CHAPTER B

1. Where there is more than one group of nutritional characteristics indicated in column 2 of Chapter A, denoted by "and/or", for the same nutritional purpose, the feeding stuff may have either or both groups in order to fulfil the nutritional purpose specified in column 1.

2. Where a group of additives is mentioned in column 2 or column 4 of Chapter A, the additive(s) used must be authorised as corresponding to the specified essential characteristic.

3. Where the source(s) of feed materials or of analytical constituents is/are required in column 4 of Chapter A the manufacturer must make a specific declaration (i.e. specific name of the feed material(s), animal species or part of the animal) allowing the evaluation of conformity of the feeding stuff with the corresponding essential nutritional characteristics.

4. Where the declaration of a substance, also authorised as an additive, is required by column 4 of Chapter A and is accompanied by the expression "total", the declared content must refer to, as appropriate, the quantity naturally present where none is added or the total quantity of the substance naturally present and the amount added as an additive.

5. The declarations specified in column 4 of Chapter A which include the words "if added" are required where the feed material or the additive has been incorporated or its content increased specifically to enable the achievement of the particular nutritional purpose.

6. The declarations to be given in accordance with column 4 of Chapter A concerning analytical constituents and additives must be expressed in quantitative terms.

7. The recommended period of use indicated in column 5 of Chapter A indicates a range within which the nutritional purpose should normally be achieved. Manufacturers may refer to more precise periods of use, within the permitted range.

8. Where a feeding stuff is intended to meet more than one particular nutritional purpose, it must comply with the corresponding entries in Chapter A.

9. In the case of a complementary feeding stuff intended for a particular nutritional purpose, guidance on the balance of the daily ration must be provided in the instructions for use.

CATEGORIES OF FEED MATERIALS FOR USE IN RELATION TO COMPOUND FEEDING STUFFS FOR PET ANIMALS

	Description of the Category	*Definition*
1.	Meat and animal derivatives	All the fleshy parts of slaughtered warm–blooded land animals fresh or preserved by appropriate treatment, and all products and derivatives of the processing of the carcase or parts of the carcase of such animals
2.	Milk and milk derivatives	All milk products, fresh or preserved by appropriate treatment and derivatives from the processing thereof
3.	Eggs and egg derivatives	All egg products fresh or preserved by appropriate treatment, and derivatives from the processing thereof
4.	Oils and fats	All animal and vegetable oils and fats
5.	Yeasts	All yeasts, the cells of which have been killed and dried
6.	Fish and fish derivatives	Fish or parts of fish, fresh or preserved by appropriate treatment, and derivatives from the processing thereof
7.	Cereals	All types of cereal, regardless of their presentation, or products made from the starchy endosperm
8.	Vegetables	All types of vegetables and legumes, fresh or preserved by appropriate treatment
9.	Derivatives of vegetable origin	Derivatives resulting from the treatment of vegetable products in particular cereals, vegetables, legumes and oil seeds
10.	Vegetable protein extracts	All products of vegetable origin in which the proteins have been concentrated by an adequate process to contain at least 50% protein, as related to the dry matter, and which may be restructured or textured
11.	Minerals	All inorganic substances suitable for animal feed
12.	Various sugars	All types of sugar
13.	Fruit	All types of fruit, fresh or preserved by appropriate treatment
14.	Nuts	All kernels from shells
15.	Seeds	All types of seeds as such or roughly crushed
16.	Algae	Algae, fresh or preserved by appropriate treatment
17.	Molluscs and crustaceans	All types of molluscs, crustaceans, shellfish, fresh or preserved by appropriate treatment, and their processing derivatives
18.	Insects	All types of insects in any stage of development
19.	Bakery products	All bread, cakes, biscuits and pasta products

SCHEDULE 9

AMENDING INSTRUMENTS REVOKED

The Feeding Stuffs and the Feeding Stuffs (Enforcement) (Amendment) (England) Regulations 2001(**a**), in so far as they amend the 2000 Regulations.

The Feeding Stuffs (Amendment) Regulations 2002(**b**), in so far as they amend the 2000 Regulations in relation to England.

The Feeding Stuffs (Amendment) Regulations 2003(**c**), in so far as they amend the 2000 Regulations in relation to England.

The Feeding Stuffs, the Feeding Stuffs (Sampling and Analysis) and the Feeding Stuffs (Enforcement) (Amendment) (England) Regulations 2003(**d**), with the exception of regulations 6 and 10(c), in so far as they amend the 2000 Regulations.

The Feeding Stuffs, the Feeding Stuffs (Sampling and Analysis) and the Feeding Stuffs (Enforcement) (Amendment) (England) (No. 2) Regulations 2003(**e**), in so far as they amend the 2000 Regulations.

The Feeding Stuffs, the Feeding Stuffs (Sampling and Analysis) and the Feeding Stuffs (Enforcement) (Amendment) (England) Regulations 2004(**f**) in so far as they amend the 2000 Regulations.

The Feeding Stuffs, the Feeding Stuffs (Sampling and Analysis) and the Feeding Stuffs (Enforcement) (Amendment) (England) (No. 2) Regulations 2004(**g**) in so far as they amend the 2000 Regulations.

(**a**) S.I. 2001/3389.
(**b**) S.I. 2002/892.
(**c**) S.I. 2003/1026.
(**d**) S.I. 2003/1503.
(**e**) S.I. 2003/2912.
(**f**) S.I. 2004/1301.
(**g**) S.I. 2004/2688.

(This note is not part of the Regulations)

1. These Regulations which apply in relation to England only—

  (a) largely revoke and replace the Feeding Stuffs Regulations 2000 as amended, ("the 2000 Regulations");

  (b) introduce new provisions to enforce and administer Regulation (EC) No. 1831/2003 on additives for use in animal nutrition ("the Additives Regulation"); and

  (c) implement Commission Directive 2004/116/EC amending the Annex to Council Directive 82/471/EEC as regards the inclusion of *Candida guilliermondii.*

They provide for the implementation or as the case may be the continuing implementation of the EC Directives and Decision listed at paragraph 11 below.

2. The Regulations apply to farmed creatures and pet animals, and in regulation 14 also to animals living freely in the wild.

3. The Regulations preserve the modifications made to the Agriculture Act 1970 ("the Act") by regulations 20 and 21 of the 2000 Regulations, with the minor drafting amendment that the definition of "pet animal" is made explicit rather than by reference to EC legislation (*regulations 3 and 4*).

4. They continue to prescribe the material that is "prescribed material" for the purposes of sections 68(1) and 69(1) of the Act as any material useable as a feeding stuff (*regulation 5*). Under those sections, sellers of prescribed materials are required to give to purchasers "statutory statements" covering the composition of the material and information on storage, handling and use. Material held for sale must be marked with such information.

5. They revoke with certain exceptions the provisions of the 2000 Regulations, which were last amended by S.I. 2004/2688, and re-enact the majority of those provisions.

6. Part 2 of these Regulations deals with the presentation and composition of feeding stuffs. The content of the statutory statement and other declarations are prescribed by *regulation 8 and Schedule 3* and their form by *regulation 9*. (The labelling of additives and premixtures not mixed with feeding stuffs is now regulated directly by Regulation (EC) No. 1831/2003).

7. The Regulations with minor drafting amendments also re-enact provisions of the 2000 Regulations so as to—

  (a) prescribe the limits of inaccuracy permitted in the declaration of ingredients (*regulation 10 and Schedule 4*);

  (b) attribute meanings to the names of certain materials for the purposes of section 70 of the Act (which creates an implicit warranty that material described by a name to which a meaning has been assigned under that section accords with the meaning (*regulation 11*);

  (c) prescribe the way in which compound feeds may be sealed and packaged (*regulation 12*);

  (d) regulate the putting into circulation and use of feed materials (*regulation 13 and Schedule 2*);

  (e) restrict the putting into circulation or use of feeding stuffs containing specified undesirable substances (*regulation 14 and Schedule 5*);

  (f) prohibit the putting into circulation or use of any feeding stuff containing certain prescribed substances (*regulation 15*);

  (g) control the marketing and use of certain protein sources and non-protein nitrogenous compounds in feeds (*regulation 16 and Schedule 6*);

  (h) regulate the iron content of milk replacer feeds (*regulation 17*);

  (i) prohibit the putting into circulation of compound feeding stuffs in which the amount of ash insoluble in hydrochloric acid exceeds specified levels (*regulation 18*); and

  (j) control the marketing of feeds intended for particular nutritional purposes (dietetics) (*regulation 19 and Schedule 7*).

8. These Regulations provide for the implementation of Commission Directive 2004/116/ EC mentioned above by including *Candida guilliermondii* among the substances authorised and regulated by *regulation 16 and Schedule 6,* and in *regulation 20* provide for the execution and enforcement of the Additives Regulation by—

(a) making it an offence not to comply with certain specified requirements in the Additives Regulation (*paragraphs (1) and (2)*);

(b) giving effect to the transitional arrangements in the Additives Regulation relating to products already on the market that were authorised under superseded EC legislation (*paragraph (3)*); and

(c) giving effect to the transitional arrangements in the Additives Regulation relating to applications for authorisation under the superseded EC legislation that were still being processed at the date of application of the Additives Regulation.

9. In relation to feed additives these Regulations also maintain the duty of confidentiality imposed by the 2000 Regulations on anyone who may, in the course of processing an application for authorisation, have acquired commercially sensitive information (*regulation 21*).

10. Part 3 of these Regulations deals with enforcement. It re-enacts provisions in the 2000 Regulations that—

(a) provide for the enforcement of requirements where the legal basis is the European Communities Act by linking such requirements to enforcement provisions in the Act (*regulation 22*);

(b) modify section 74A of the Act and provide for offences and penalties in relation to matters covered by the Regulations that would not otherwise come within that section (*regulation 23*); and

(c) amend, in relation to England, the Feeding Stuffs (Sampling and Analysis) Regulations 1999 in the same way as that expressed as a modification in the 2000 Regulations, and also make consequential amendments to the 1999 Regulations mentioned above (*regulation 24*).

11. The EC Directives implemented by these Regulations are—

(a) Council Directive 70/524/EEC (OJ No. L270, 14.12.70, p. 1) concerning additives in feedingstuffs, (to the extent that its measures are preserved by Regulation (EC) No. 1831/2003), as last amended by Council Regulation (EC) No. 1756/2002 (OJ No. L265, 3.10.2002, p. 1);

(b) Council Directive 79/373/EEC (OJ No. L86, 6.4.79, p. 30) on the circulation of compound feedingstuffs, as last amended by Council Regulation (EC) No. 807/2003 (OJ No. L122, 16.5.2003, p. 36);

(c) Council Directive 82/471/EEC (OJ No. L213, 21.7.82, p. 8) concerning certain products used in animal nutrition, as last amended by Commission Directive 2004/ 116/EC (OJ No. L379, 24.12.2004, p. 81);

(d) Council Directive 93/74/EEC (OJ No. L237, 22.9.93, p. 23) on feedingstuffs intended for particular nutritional purposes, as last amended by Council Regulation (EC) No. 806/2003 (OJ No. L122, 16.5.2003, p. 1);

(e) Commission Directive 94/39/EC (OJ No. L207, 10.8.94, p. 20) establishing a list of intended uses of animal feedingstuffs for particular nutritional purposes;

(f) Council Directive 96/25/EC (OJ No. L125, 23.5.96, p. 35) on the circulation and use of feed materials, as last amended by Council Regulation (EC) No. 806/2003 (OJ No. L122, 16.5.2003, p. 1);

(g) Directive 2002/32/EC of the European Parliament and of the Council (OJ No. L140, 30.5.2002, p. 10) on undesirable substances in animal feed, as last amended by Commission Directive 2003/100/EC (OJ No. L285, 1.11.2003, p. 33); and

(h) Commission Decision 2004/217/EC adopting a list of materials whose circulation or use for animal nutrition purposes is prohibited (OJ No. L67, 5.3.2004, p. 31).

12. A full regulatory impact assessment of the effect that this instrument will have on the costs of business has been prepared and placed in the Library of each House of Parliament together with a transposition note setting out how the provisions of Commission Directive 2004/116/EC have been transposed into domestic law by these Regulations. Copies may be obtained from the Primary Production Division of the Food Standards Agency, Aviation House, 125 Kingsway, London WC2B 6NH.

S T A T U T O R Y   I N S T R U M E N T S

2005 No. 3281

AGRICULTURE

The Feeding Stuffs (England) Regulations 2005